The Steely Dan File

By Stephen V. O'Rourke

© 2007 Stephen V. O'Rourke

All rights reserved.

Library of Congress Cataloging–In-Publication Data

O'Rourke, Stephen V. 1962-

The Steely Dan File/ Stephen V. O'Rourke

p. cm.

Includes discography, bibliography, chronology and footnotes

1 Steely Dan (aka Donald Fagen & Walter Becker)- Biography 2. Musicians- United States-Biography 3. Rock groups- United States- chronology

No Part of this book may be reproduced or transmitted in any form or by any means, electronic or mechanical, including photocopying or recording, or by any information storage and retrieval system, without written permission from the author

ISBN 978-0-6151-7299-6

LCCN

Printed in the United States of America.

The Steely Dan File
The Steely Dan File
The Steely Dan File
The Steely Dan File
The Steely Dan File
The Steely Dan File

The Steely Dan File

From Naked Lunch to Morph the Cat

If you had told someone back in 1972 that Steely Dan would still be around 35 years later, touring and issuing new music, they would probably think you were as whacked out as Billy Burroughs was when he wrote Naked Lunch. From its inception Steely Dan was working against the odds, going against the grain. Gifted students of American bohemia, intellectuals in a world of substance abuse, they managed to collaborate, compromise and perform magnificently at the close of the hippie era in the early '70s. Like a supernova the original Steely Dan splashed onto the American consciousness with a Gold album and #1 single withing six months of its debut in the fall of '72. As Watergate unfolded on the frontpage Steely Dan sneaked onto the entertainment pages of American newspapers in 1973, playing concerts everywhere from Louisiana to Des Moines to Salt Lake City. Although touring in those days was brutal and not profitable it helped sear Steely Dan into the minds of high school and college kids of middle America and create lifelong devotees. When they gave up touring in 1974 Steely Dan were declaring freedom! Artistic freedom to compose, record and dabble as needed….Their floating workshop unshackled the rock industry and paved the way for the future of the recording industry. After the public got a taste of pop perfection in 1977 with *Aja* there was no going back. When Donald Fagen put out the perfect bookend to *Aja* five years later with his solo disc '*The Nightfly*'…we were on hallowed ground…..someone had managed to create studio

The Steely Dan File

precision and mixed it up with imagination and heart. Steely Dan fans could rock out...but it was all in the mind...we didn't need to impress...with flash and all the trappings of rock n roll clichés....but it would be another decade before we could hear it all live again. In 1993 when Steely Dan reformed and began doing concerts again the crtitics and cynics were back in force...the odds were stacke high against Fagen and Becker....but with a ton of songs that had yet be performed live a Steely Dan concert during the Clinton Administration was a reward to the faithful and the survivors. The boys could actually play and many of the songs were revealed to be American classics that stood up to the test of time and benefited from new arrangements. Like characters in their own songs Steely Dan morphed into 21st Century creations, putting out brilliant new tracks in 2000, 2003 and 2006…..really good music is like a drug, and sometimes it's better to just DO IT, rather than think about the implications….thankfully Steely Dan has done it for the past 35 years….and the world is a better place for it. Buroughs once said Steely Dan had "Too Many Horses Heads"….ha! These boys are having the last laugh….

Stephen Vincent O'Rourke
Singapore

Contents

I The Grateful Dead of Beverly Blvd — 1
II The Floating Workshop — 49
III True Companions — 91
IV Back To 'Nature — 117

Appendixes
Discography — 145
Chronology — 159
Bibliography — 181

The Steely Dan File

1

The Grateful Dead of Beverly Blvd.

1971-1975

The Steely Dan File

The Grateful Dead of Beverly Boulevard

*W*hen *Steely Dan was first put* together in late 1971 they were very much the right band, *at the right time.* The music scene at that time was a melting pot of diversity. Isaac Hayes' black funk of 'Shaft' saddled right next to John Lennon's minimalistic 'Imagine' in the Top 10. Classic hits by Sly and the Family Stone, Cat Stevens, Chicago and Marvin Gaye stood alongside forgettable hits of the day by David Cassidy, The Osmonds and Bread.

One record company that typified the music scene in the early 1970's was ABC Dunhill Records. Formed in the mid-sixties by Los Angeles music executive Lou Adler, Dun-

The Steely Dan File

hill Records had gone from strength to strength with super selling acts like the Mommas and Poppas, Steppenwolf and Three Dog Night

In late 1971 while it was celebrating yet another Top 40 hit from Three Dog Night ('An Old fashioned Love Song') it was also suffering through such chart bombs like 'For Ladies Only' by Steppenwolf (#74), 'Mammy Blue' by the Pop-Tops (#68) and 'My Boy' by Richard Harris (#95).

Luckily for fledgling New York songwriters Donald Fagen and Walter Becker ABC Dunhill was not standing still in the competitive sweepstakes that made up the music scene of the early 1970's. In fact ABC executives were in the process of hiring new producers, new rock bands and new songwriters. The potential was there for something big to emerge and when Gary Katz, friend and mentor to the songwriters Walter Becker and Donald Fagen, landed a job as record producer at ABC Dunhill in November of 1971 the stage was set. The music industry would never be the same

The Land of Milk and Honey

After floundering around in their native New York area for the better part of three years the two beat personas of Donald J.

The Grateful Dead of Beverly Boulevard

Fagen and Walter C. Becker had landed staff songwriting positions at ABC Dunhill Records in Los Angeles. Their friend and confidante Gary Katz had gotten them the job after he himself had been hired by the label as a staff producer on the recommendation of executive Eddie Lambert. Things moved quickly and by November 1971 the songwriters were already relocated and writing for ABC Dunhill rock bands. By December they had even begun recording the first *Steely Dan* demos[1], after hours, at the newly constructed ABC Recording Studios.

The man building the studios was audio engineer Roger Nichols[2] and he along with Katz would remain as cornerstones for much of the Steely Dan saga over the next several decades. A native of Oakland in northern California, Nichols' family eventually relocated to the Los Angeles area where the young Nichols would be a high school chum of future enigmatic rock persona Frank Zappa. Nichols himself was an audiologist

---

[1] It is uncertain exactly when the first recording sessions for Steely Dan took place-but in the 1993 booklet for Citizen Dan, (the MCA Box Set), Fagen & Becker indicated that the demo of 'Everyones Gone To The Movies' was recorded close to a year before the release of Steely Dan's debut album Can't Buy A Thrill.

[2] Steely Dan's Roger Nichols is not the Roger Nichols who recorded and wrote songs for A&M Records during this same period, most notably 'Close To You'.

The Steely Dan File

and hi-fi proponent and would lend his hand to the first Steely Dan recordings in December of 1971, demo recordings of the songs 'Everyone's Gone To The Movies' and 'Sail The Waterway'.

By early 1972 ABC Dunhill Record executives were actively looking for something new. When their leading hard rock band Steppenwolf announced that they were breaking, up a new sense of urgency came over them to locate *the next big thing*. They were open to ideas for new bands.

Gary Katz saw his opportunity and seized it. ABC executives, led by Steve Barri and Eddie Lambert gave a limited go ahead for Steely Dan to record. They needed to convince tough label president Jay Lasker that the Becker/Fagen sound was something special and something that would sell. Over the course of the late 1960's ABC Dunhill had become a major player in the pop singles market with million selling acts like Three Dog Night, the Grass Roots and the Mommas & the Poppas. There was a distinct sound to many ABC records and the label prided itself on its track record.

Initial response to Steely Dan when they recorded their first songs was mixed. Their first record, 'Dallas', was issued briefly in March of 1972 (June in the UK), but it

The Grateful Dead of Beverly Boulevard

didn't blow anyone away with its odd combination of pedal steel and congas. But it sounded like the boys had talent and with the right tweaking and personnel something could and should come out of it. In April of 1972 ABC Records offered Steely Dan a recording contract to record a full-length album, subject to approval.

Thus began the life of Steely Dan the musical entity. Taking the name from the controversial avant-garde beat novel by William S. Burroughs, *Naked Lunch*, songwriters Walter Becker and Donald Fagen were destined to leave an imprint on the decade of the 1970's in a way no other musical act of the period could. These guys were intellectuals in the days of "tune in, turn on & drop out". Be-boppers in the days of glam and prog rock.

From their obscure musical industry origins (i.e. The soundtrack to the counter-culture film by Peter Locke, 'You Gotta Walk It, Like You Talk It', touring as members of Jay and the Americans etc)[3] and their equally

---

[3] When the soundtrack to 'You Gotta Walk...' was actually recorded is uncertain, but it was defintely recorded some time before its September 1971 release on Spark Records. Brian Sweets 1994 book Reeling In The Years gives a detailed account on the making of the film and Fagen and Becker's contribution to it

The Steely Dan File

obscure connections to jazz session players (i.e. Victor Feldman) Fagen and Becker would create an entity that was distinct for its' times. No major connections to the 1960's, no psychedelia, no heavy metal, no posturing art-rock, Steely Dan harkened back to an earlier and more obscure period. They were cool, yet corny, sophisticated, yet simple, professional yet uncertain...but they were always good. You would always get your moneys' worth when purchasing a record that bore the name Steely Dan.

A Name You will Never Forget

Not unlike other recording acts that had produced hit records for ABC Dunhill[4] Steely Dan was very much an enigma from its' inception. Initiated in secret at the offices of ABC Dunhill after business hours, the group was led by a pair of sarcastic college buddies: the 25 year old Victor Mature look alike Donald J. Fagen and his sly wordsmith of a

---
[4] In fact the group which Fagen and Becker were first assigned to compose songs for, The Grass Roots, originated around recordings made by singer-songwriter PF Sloan and songwriter/executive Steve Barri, only later was an actual band brought in to perform the songs live. Barri and Sloan had previously made it big with their hit 'Secret Agent Man' by Johnny Rivers.

The Grateful Dead of Beverly Boulevard

colleague Walter C. Becker, all of 23. Both hailed from the New York City area and had met and began writing at Bard College in upstate New York in 1967.

Fagen, a native of northern New Jersey, was born in Passaic on January 10, 1948. His father Joseph "Jay" Fagen was an accountant and hailed from a long line of Fagen's from the Jersey City area. Fagen's mother Eleanor Rosenberg was Jewish (with eastern European roots) and hailed from New York City. Fagen's mother was in many ways Donald Fagen's role model as a singer and performer, having been the "Shirley Temple of the Catskills"[5]- a child singer in the 1930's and '40's. One bad case of stage fright at the age of 15 however ended the young Eleanor's career. She married Joseph Fagen in 1947 and two years after Donald Fagen's birth, a daughter Susan was born.

Growing up in Kendall Park, New Jersey Fagen showed talent for the piano at an early age and by the age of 15 was an accomplished self-taught player. His parents pushed him to college and he eventually undertook a musical evaluation at Princeton and was accepted. Always an *'out of the box'* thinker however, the young Fagen had al-

---

[5] What Rhymes With Orange Alert? By Fred Kaplan NY Times February 26, 2006

ready decided that he didn't want to learn music formally. He wanted to emulate the jazz hero's of his record collection: Red Garland, Thelonious Monk....Bud Powell. Listening to jazz radio stations broadcasting out of New York, like WNCN, WEVD and WRVR the teenage Fagen had already formed a beat like persona that would color his vision for much of his musical career.

After turning down a chance to attend the prestigious Princeton, Fagen turned his interest north and enrolled in the upstate New York college of Bard, located in the town of Annandale-on the Hudson about forty miles north of Manhattan. For a brief period Fagen would also attend Berklee School of Music in Boston but his main source for higher education was Bard- the onetime site of a Lutheran seminary known as St. Stephen's.

By the 1960's Bard and its surrounding area was something of a counter-culture haven. Nearby lived Bob Dylan, The Band.... Timothy Leary. Attending Bard itself in the mid sixties was an array of characters who would eventually attain fame elsewhere. Actress Blythe Danner was there with her boyfriend, future actor-comedian Chevy Chase, folk singer Terence Boylan was there

The Grateful Dead of Beverly Boulevard

as was Fagen's future wife, Libby Titus, a future dancer and concert promoter[6].

Chevy Chase was an aspiring drummer while at Bard and he remembered Fagen well, "He'd walk around with this beak of a nose and he always wore black clothing and looked down with his hands in his pockets. People thought he was kind of weird and quiet. They didn't realize that he was really intelligent, a very funny, bright guy." Eventually Chase would team up with Fagen in one of the many pick-up bands that Fagen would form. As Becker remembered, "Donald was the dean of the pick-up band syndrome at Bard, the bands we came up with sounded like a cross between the Kingsmen and Zappa[7]."

Walter Becker began attending classes at Bard in the fall of 1967 at the tender age of 17. A graduate of Stuyvesant High School in Manhattan, Walter Carl Becker was born in Westchester, New York on February 10,

---

[6] Boylan was a star in his own right by the time he began attending Bard, having made a name for himself as a sort of New York version of Bob Dylan, playing at coffee houses in the mid-sixties. In 1968 he secured a deal with MGM Records. His brother Rick Boylan was a songwriter himself and eventually became a prominent persona in the Southern California folk rock scene with figures like JD Souther, Jackson Browne and the Eagles et al.

[7] Liner notes to *You Gotta Walk It Like You Talk It*, 1978 JEM Records

The Steely Dan File

1950. Becker's father died of a heart attack in 1965 and the teenager took solace from his music. Like Fagen, Becker grew up listening to jazz radio and counted among his favorites Charlie Parker, Miles Davis and John Coltrane. Also like Fagen, Becker was a literary buff, particularly of beat writers like Kerouac, Ginsberg and Burroughs. Unlike Fagen, Becker found it hard to sustain his studies at Bard and in 1968 was asked to withdraw due to "lack of seriousness to the work study program[8]."

Fagen and Becker's college days would become mythologized in some of their early Steely Dan lyrics and it wasn't a happy ride all the way through. In the spring of 1969, at the height of the "us versus them" era in the counter-culture sixties- Bard experienced a major police raid on their frat houses and dormitories. A large group of students, including Fagen and Becker were rounded up, arrested and thoroughly humiliated. Fagen, among others, even had his head shaven.

At his graduation ceremony in June of '69, Fagen protested by refusing to sit with his class, even though he graduated with high marks and a BA in English Literature. Becker meanwhile, had also been arrested in

---

[8]   ibid.

The Grateful Dead of Beverly Boulevard

the raid, but had relocated back to New York and waited for Fagen to join him in a pursuit of songwriting career in Manhattan.

Two of Becker's friends in Queens were accomplished guitarists and had gained a certain amount of fame even before Becker had met Fagen and started the Steely Dan journey. One of his friends was an Ohio transplant named Rick Zheringer who had scored a Gold single with his garage band the Real McCoys ('Hang On Sloopy'). He would later gain fame as Rick Derringer and begin collaborating with Steely Dan in 1973 when he was at the height of his fame as a solo artist and as a member of the Edgar Winter Band.

Becker's other New York friend was a teenage phenome named Randy Wolfe. Wolfe would team up with his stepfather, Ed Cassidy, and launch the legendary band Spirit in 1968. Christened Randy "California" by none other than Jimi Hendrix, Wolfe had a genuine bluesy style that Becker used as reference for his early guitar playing days.

Becker's guitar playing aspirations however would take a back seat upon leaving Bard as he and Fagen launched the Steely Dan game plan in 1969. Becker and Fagen would be songwriters first; and if need be they would be background musicians second.

The Steely Dan File

When Fagen and Becker secured positions with the group Jay & the Americans in the summer of 1969 Becker and Fagen toured with the band as bass player and keyboardist respectively, positions they would continue to take when they initiated Steely Dan in 1971. They also worked as the bands staff composers and horn arrangers.

Jay & The Americans were mainly a vocal act, a sort of poor man's Four Seasons, and had scored only one major US hit, 'Cara Mia' in 1965. Their leader, Jay Black, was a cocky, sort of guy, reputed to have Mafia connections. Fagen and Becker's days with the band were a humorous "excellent" adventure that gave the composers a peak into the dark side of both the music industry and the touring circuit.

In many ways Fagen and Becker were catching a glimpse of the end of the Brill Building era and that glimpse would provide them with a model on how they themselves would do business. Their early experiences in New York gave them a sort of east coast music industry sensibility that would sustain them in the long years ahead on the west coast.

Their mentor at ABC Dunhill and the man who had gotten them hired was another person with east coast savvy, Brooklyn na-

The Grateful Dead of Beverly Boulevard

tive Gary Katz, who for a brief period was an aspiring singer under the name of Gary Kannon[9]. In New York, Katz had worked for various record labels and production companies with limited success and had met Becker and Fagen while working on an abortive record for singer Linda Hoover at MGM Records. It was at these sessions that the original discussions for creating a band like Steely Dan had come up.[10]

With the idea of setting up a "Steely Dan" type band, with Fagen and Becker at the helm, Katz got himself hired as a staff producer for ABC Dunhill Records in late 1971. On the phone to ABC executive Steve Barri, Katz pleaded that his songwriting friends be hired, site unseen, along with himself.

So sure of their talent Katz vowed to resign from his own position as staff producer if Fagen and Becker weren't a success within two or three years. Barri was impressed with Katz' *chutzpah* and agreed to hire the songwriting duo; initially just to write pop songs

---

[9] Katz' name in fact appears as Gary Kannon, as producer, on the very first Steely Dan record, 'Dallas'. He also appears as a backing vocalist on several ABC Records as Gary Kannon.

[10] Becker and Fagen's first studio session work also came at MGM Records. They assisted Terence Boylan on his 1970 release Alias Boona.

The Steely Dan File

for ABC Dunhill's roster of acts, which included at that time, the Grass Roots, John Kaye, Three Dog Night and Jimmy Buffett.

Soon after their arrival however it became apparent to all involved that Fagen and Becker's material was less suited for existing acts than for an entirely new vehicle. Thus was borne The *Dan of Steel*. In the end only a few Fagen and Becker songs were ever recorded by non-Steely Dan groups. John Kaye, the former leader of Steppenwolf, recorded "Giles of the River", Poco recorded "Dallas", Denny Doherty, ex-lead singer of the Momma's and the Poppa's, recorded "Sail the Waterway'. Folk rocker Thomas Jefferson Kaye (aka Tommy Kaye) recorded two Fagen and Becker songs in 1973, 'Jones' and 'American Lover'. The Texas rockers Narasota recorded 'Canyon Ladies' for their 1972 debut, while the all female northern California based Birtha recorded 'Dirty Work' on their 1973 album. None of these recordings were memorable and it would be some 25 years before any substantive attempt would be made to record any Fagen and Becker songs by major rock artists[11].

---

[11] The soundtrack for the film *'Me Myself & Irene'* (in 2000) featured artists Brian Setzer, Smashmouth & Wilco performing Steely Dan songs, some famous, some not.

The Grateful Dead of Beverly Boulevard

AMERICA'S UNLIKELIEST SUPERGROUP

One by one Katz called in new potential members of the band. From New York would come guitarist Jeff Baxter, affectionately nicknamed "Skunk", and from Boston came drummer and vocalist Jim Hodder, whom Katz had worked with before in a band named Bead Game[12]. Becker and Fagen themselves were already penciled in as bass and keyboard players for the new band and would be continually on the look out for new players that might enhance the Steely Dan sound.

When they first signed their contract to record an album in April of 1972[13] they immediately placed a call to Long Island, New York, home of guitarist Denny Dias. Dias was

---

[12] Cambridge based Bead Game featured Hodder on lead vocals and drums and recorded one album for Avco Embassy Records in 1970 and were part of the Boston Sound, they had one hit single (Sweet Medusa [Avco embassy 4539]) and appeared in the counter-culture film classic *The People Next Door*. Baxter himself was a one-time member of the cult Boston ensemble The Ultimate Spinach and was given the nickname of "Skunk" by his roommate Geoff Lyall aka Klaus Fluoride, future member of the Dead Kennedys.

[13] Although they had qualms about the contract, particularly the part about touring, Fagen and Becker signed the deal. It would be a decision that would haunt them in the years ahead but in 1972 "it was like a dream come true"-Becker 1977 interview, Cameron Crowe, Rolling Stone

The Steely Dan File

a med-school drop out who'd previously worked with the composers in a band called Demian and on the ill-fated film soundtrack of *'You Gotta Walk It Like You Talk It or You'll Lose That Beat'*, the 1971 film produced by Fagen and Becker's Bard College classmate Peter Locke.

A native of Philadelphia, Denny Dias was a horse of a different color in the hard rock scene of the early 1970's. A formally trained guitarist[14] with a jazzy be-bop flavor he would remain a close confidant of Fagen and Becker in the years ahead. A robust bearded hipster, usually attired in overalls, Dias would later be called "a refugee from Black Oak Arkansas"[15] by a critic while the entire band would slammed as "the ugliest rock band in the world" during their first tour[16].

---

[14] Dias was trained by jazz guitarist Billy Bauer. Bauer recorded a jazz classic for Verve in the mid-1950's called, *The Plectorist*, he'd previously worked with "cool" legend Lennie Tristano

[15] The Rolling Stone History of Rock & Roll (1980 edition)

[16] Citizen Steely Dan booklet c.1993 MCA Records

The Grateful Dead of Beverly Boulevard

From New York City Katz brought in yet another guitarist for the 1972 sessions, long-time friend of both Walter Becker and Jeff Baxter, Elliot Randall. Despite declining an offer to formally join the band Randall did contribute greatly to the early Steely Dan sound. His two solos on 'Reeling In the Years' were perfect and in the years ahead would be viewed as perhaps the best ever recorded on a pop record. Led Zeppelin's Jimmy Page, no slouch himself on guitar lauded Steely Dan's early stuff and named Randall's solo on 'Reelin' his favorite guitar solo of all time[17].

Aside from their rock cronies Steely Dan also managed to bring in some classy jazz players in their early sessions. Jerome Richardson, Ray Brown and Victor Feldman all made vital contributions on early Steely Dan tracks and would be the first of a long line of jazz greats to grace the songs of Fagen and Becker during the 1970's.

They stumbled on enlisting Victor Feldman quite by accident when they noticed his name on the drum kit outside the recording studio of a fellow ABC Records recording act. "We used to see cases in the hall", commented Becker years later, "and saw Victor Feldman's name. I said 'Wow, Vic-

---

[17] Reeling In The Years by Brian Sweet (OmniBus 1994)

The Steely Dan File

tor Feldman's in there, from Miles Davis and Cannon Ball Adderly."[18]

Feldman, as Becker noted had played with Miles and Cannon Ball Adderly, and he was to strike a resounding chord in the life of Steely Dan, the musical entity. Also serving as a role model of sorts to Fagen and Becker, Feldman was a hugely talented pianist and percussionist who shunned publicity for the secretively appreciated world of session work. A child prodigy from England, Feldman had once sat in on drums for Glenn Miller's ensemble at the age of ten. Relocating to Los Angeles in the late '50's he delved into life as a session player as a vibraphonist, pianist and drummer. A one time member of Woody Herman's Thundering Herd, Feldman apparently loved the studio life so much that he even turned down an offer to join Miles Davis' quintet when the famed trumpeter offered him a full time gig in the early '60's.

Aside from both Fagen and Becker, Feldman was the only person to appear on every Steely Dan album from 1972 through 1980. Along with Baxter's tight 'spanish' guitar sound, Feldman created a hypnotic "sturm and drang" of Latin percussion on 'Do

---

[18] Downbeat 6/2003, p.42

The Grateful Dead of Beverly Boulevard

it Again', destined to become the groups first hit in late 1972.

Despite their jazz connections rock 'n roll was what Steely Dan was going to play and to complete the touring entourage Fagen lobbied for another singer to be added, if only to handle the spotlight of the live performance. Katz and ABC executives were reluctant; Fagen's voice was distinctive and was already featured on the bulk of the material recorded, including the planned debut single 'Do It Again'. Fagen was insistent however and through drummer Jimmy Hodder New Jersey native David Palmer was tracked down and hired, sight unseen, as the groups new lead singer, circa July 1972.

As the album was almost complete upon his arrival Palmer's input would be limited to two tracks as lead singer ('Dirty Work' and 'Brooklyn') but he did add backing vocals to most of the other tracks, including the brilliant high harmonies on *'Reelin In The Years'*. Another track Palmer sang lead on in 1972 was 'Pearl of the Quarter', a beautiful, melodic southern ode to New Orleans. When the final studio recording of this track emerged in 1973 however Fagen had taken over the lead vocals on this early 'Dan classic.

Palmer's David Crosby influenced sound would at times, (along with Baxter's pedal steel), place Steely Dan in the folk-rock

The Steely Dan File

genre, nicely embodied in the 'Dan's Malibu rivals The Eagles, as well as Steely Dan's label mates Poco[19]. In concert Palmer would attempt to be the band's front man, handling virtually all of the lead vocal chores in addition to helping out on percussion. At times this was not a pretty sight[20].

After Palmer's tracks were recorded Katz and Nichols mixed the album and pitched it to ABC Dunhill executives for final approval and secure a release date. In addition to the Steely Dan album Katz had also been working on a hard rock album by the Texas band named Narasota and had enlisted Fagen and Becker as studio players and songwriters (they wrote one song for the album, 'Canyon Ladies') to complete it.

After ABC Dunhill gave the green light to both of these releases Katz brought in al-

---

[19] The common thread through the Eagles, Steely Dan and Poco was vocalist Timothy B. Schmitt. Schmitt contributed backing vocals for Steely Dan , essentially replacing David Palmer, on several important tracks; 1974's 'Rikki, Don't Lose That Number', 1977's 'Aja' and 1978's 'FM (No Static At All)'.

[20] Steely Dan had more than a few Spinal Tap episodes in their early days. At their first gig in Philadelphia (Nov.1972) Palmer was essentially too inerberated to sing properly and basically slurred his way through a 40 minute set.

The Grateful Dead of Beverly Boulevard

most the entire Steely Dan entourage to record his next production, a solo effort from legendary folk-rock singer Tommy Kaye. Kaye's albums were not big sellers for ABC Dunhill but they were important works that connected Steely Dan to a unique acid-folk scene, perhaps best embodied by Gram Parsons, Gene Clark and the early days of the Eagles. Like Katz, Kaye had a long resume of record industry work[21] and his two ABC solo albums stand as a unique snapshot into the final days of the of hippie-dom. Famed rock critic Robert Christgau called Fagen and Becker's 'American Lovers', "a bitter, poignant farewell to the counterculture" [22].

Neither Kaye's nor Narasota's albums would do anything near what the Steely Dan album would achieve and Katz would essentially be noted for his award winning Steely Dan work in the years ahead. Roger Nichols likewise would forever be associated with Steely Dan and his brilliant and exacting re-

---

[21] Kaye in fact was the head of Sceptre Records at the age of 18. Also working at the 1973 session for Kaye's lp's were fellow Fagen/Becker associates Kenny Vanceand Marty Kupersmith, as well as the legendary Dusty Springfield.

[22] Christgau, a writer for the Village Voice, was a big fan of Steely Dan and their related projects. To read his 1974 review of Kaye's album see this webpage=http://www.robertchristgau.com/get_artist.php?id=1578&name=Thomas+Jefferson+Kaye

The Steely Dan File

cording style would be a standard that many would emulate, few duplicate.

By September of 1972 Steely Dan's debut, the sarcastically titled *Can't Buy A Thrill*, would hit the record stores. Sporting a bizarre cover of an old snapshot of French prostitutes lined up on the street, a pair of full smiling female lips, a semi-nude muscleman and a swirling phallic symbol that stretched underneath a huge cursive script of the band's name *Can't Buy A Thrill* was popular from the get go: debuting on Cashbox's lp chart a few weeks after its' release at #149.[23]

A month after Steely Dan's lp chart debut an edited version of the lp's opening track, 'Do It Again' would enter the US singles chart and after a few well received concerts in LA and New York[24] Steely Dan, the obscure east coast band named for a dildo in Burroughs' cult novel, was on its

---

[23] Cashbox 10/15/72. *Can't Buy A Thrill* would peak at #7 on the Cashbox album chart in the spring of 1973. Billboard placed it only as high as #17.

[24] In fact Steely Dan would play for an entire week, Nov.1-7 at the famed underground club Max's Kansas City in Manhattan. Their first official concert was Oct. 1, 1972 in Seattle.

The Grateful Dead of Beverly Boulevard

way. Steely Dan had become LA's new *"show biz kids"*.

STEELY DAN 1972 RELEASES

- **Dallas/ Sail The Waterway**- (March 1972) Though not an AM radio hit, Dallas became popular with progressive FM outlets when it was released in the spring of '72. Since it was never included on any Steely Dan album it became a collector's item and is the only Steely Dan single that did not feature Donald Fagen on lead vocals, drummer Jim Hodder taking that role. Fagen does take lead vocal on the adolescent charmer 'Sail The Waterway', which features some tasty guitar work by Jeff Baxter.
- **Do It Again (edited)/ Fire In The Hole**- (November 1972) A classic track of the 1970's Do It Again put Steely Dan on the map in both the AM Top 40 world and the FM counter-culture scene. A huge hit single, hitting #1 on Record World, Do It Again would be covered by many artists Fagen and Becker would still be using it as a concert highlight when they toured in the late '90's and it remains a staple on classic rock radio stations to this day.

The Steely Dan File

CAN'T BUY A THRILL (OCTOBER 1972)
A surprising hit album, Can't Buy A Thrill, was released with little fanfare in the fall of 1972 and became a Gold Record by early 1973. It was a hodgepodge of sounds. From funky urban Latin shuffles on 'Do It Again' to the Crosby, Stills & Nash influence of 'Reelin In The Years' the album represented the conflicting sounds championed by the original members of the band. While Steely Dan's version of Eagles-esque rock was unique and interesting it would ultimately lose out to the urban jazz grooves so loved by the composers. Can't Buy A Thrill and its two sequels represent a brief and brilliant chapter of the 'Dan's pedal-steel/acoustic jamboree. Now consummately re-mastered on compact disc this bright debut set still conjures up clear images of LA 1972.

Rating: 1 2 3 4 5 6 7 **8** 9 10

The Grateful Dead of Beverly Boulevard

They Got the Steely Dan T-shirt

The year 1973 was to be a pivotal year in the careers of Walter Becker and Donald Fagen. It laid the cornerstone for the Platinum hits that lay ahead and provided both of them with enough anecdotes to be used in interviews years later. Not your usual run-of-the-mill rock band Steely Dan would become what Rolling Stone magazine would call "America's unlikeliest Supergroup"[25].

The surprisingly quick success of both the single 'Do It Again' and the album *Can't Buy A Thrill* caused a bit of a panic in the band when they realized that a full nationwide tour was in order to satisfy their new found audience. 'Do It Again' proved to be a hugely popular hit, breaking into Billboard's Top 10 in February of 1973, eventually selling close to a million copies.

"The entire continent seems to be whistling that catchy Steely Dan hit.', noted rock critic Ritchie Yorke[26]. The success of 'Do It Again' was a proud achievement for a pair of

---

[25] Rolling Stone 8/15/74 'Steely Dan Comes Up Swinging' by Charles Perry

[26] Winnipeg Free Press March 7, 1973

The Steely Dan File

songwriters who'd only a year previous had virtually nothing to show for their unique composing skills. The album likewise was a huge success peaking at #7 on the US albums charts[27].

Through the ABC Records hierarchy a publicity campaign was launched to promote their new *super group* Steely Dan. In January the group appeared on Dick Clark's American Bandstand and "performed" 'Do It Again' and for the hip older hard rock crowd they taped a live segment for the NBC's new rock show, the Midnight Special. Steely Dan was in fact featured on the program's debut episode, which aired in early February just as 'Do It Again' was peaking in the US Top 10. Sales for *Can't Buy A Thrill* were also increasing and the album broke into Billboard's album Top 40 chart on February 10, 1973.

This two pronged approached would serve Steely Dan well in the years ahead. They were one of the few groups to chart regularly on the lp charts as well in the Top 40 bubble gum world, with shrewdly edited versions of their lp's bouncier pop tracks.

Under the direction of Three Dog Night manager Joel Cohen, who was assigned to

---

[27] Record World May 1973

The Grateful Dead of Beverly Boulevard

manage the band by ABC executives, Steely Dan stepped into the limelight and began its first headlining tour in April of 1973, having previously performed as an opening act for the Kinks, The James Gang and Elton John, among many others. Cohen was from the formulized school of touring: i.e. release singles and tour to promote them....regularly. So with the release of their next single, 'Reeling In The Years', Fagen and Becker got on that rock 'n roll treadmill they'd held in distain from the start and had studiously attempted to avoid. Their apprehensions would prove to be correct but for a brief period Steely Dan was a bustling band of six, later dubbed "the Grateful Dead of Beverly Boulevard" by Becker himself.[28]

Touring with fellow classic rockers the Doobie Brothers and the mellow folk duo Seals and Crofts, Steely Dan toured the US for much of the spring and summer of 1973, only taking a break to work on the recording of their second album *Countdown To Ecstasy*.

The very first band that Steely Dan had toured with had been the Cleveland rockers The James Gang, led at the time by the future Eagle Joe Walsh and guitarist

---

[28] Becker, interview with Robert W. Morgan, (1978 Westwood Radio/WPLR-FM Stamford, CT) "We were the Grateful Dead of Beverly Boulevard....we were very strange."

The Steely Dan File

extraordinaire Domenic Troiano. Troiano had become a favorite of Fagen and Becker's after they had heard him jamming at a Gary Katz session circa 1970. Troiano had an elegant style that Fagen thought would be perfect for the original Steely Dan. In fact he had even been offered a spot in the original 'Dan lineup but turned it down, like a few other notables had.[29]

Can't Buy A Thrill meanwhile would remain high on the LP charts for much of the year and yield a 2nd Top 20 hit in the folk-rock influenced 'Reeling In The Years'. 'Reeling' was another bonafide smash, hitting #7 in Cashbox, #11 in Billboard and #1 in Variety. Success record-sales wise however would lead to the first signs of friction between the composers and their record company.

Sensing that they may have another pop music hit making machine; in the tradition of Three Dog Night, Steppenwolf and The Grass Roots, ABC Records pressed Becker and Fagen for an immediate new (i.e. non-*Can't Buy A Thrill*) single to be used for to promote Steely Dan's summer tour.

---

[29] Others who turned down an invitation to join Steely Dan include Elliot Randall and Chevy Chase.

The Grateful Dead of Beverly Boulevard

Showing some of the tongue-in-cheek cynicism they'd become notorious for Fagen and Becker responded with a quirky, off kiltered track entitled 'Show Biz Kids'. Lyrically a scathing put down of both L.A. and the overall show business of the record industry, 'Show Biz Kids' featured a wicked slide guitar from Rick Derringer. Released as a single in July of 1973 'Kids struggled weakly up the singles chart as AM disc-jockeys, expecting another 'Reeling In the Years', found difficulty in adding it to their tight bubblegum playlists.

Consequently Steely Dan's second album, *Countdown To Ecstasy* didn't sell nearly as well as its predecessor. Despite excellent reviews the album only reached #35 on the Billboard LP chart and stayed in the Top 40 for only 3 weeks. 'Show Biz Kids' likewise had sluggish sales and failed to break Billboard's magical Top 40 barrier, although it did managed to reach #31 in Cashbox.

It was a slightly different Steely Dan that recorded *Countdown To Ecstasy,* with lead singer David Palmer being quietly sacked at the end of the spring tour[30]. Fagen

---

[30] During their early tours Fagen and Becker did make an effort to change Steely Dan's sound to be more in stride with Palmer's vocals; several new songs were written just for him and others re-arranged to suit him better. In fact, at least one concert in Salt Lake City was

The Steely Dan File

was now resigned to his fate as Steely Dan's main voice, but when they began touring again in August three additional singers were enlisted to help out with the somewhat difficult vocal chores.

Royce Jones, who'd met drummer Jim Hodder at a party in Hollywood, effectively took over Palmer's spot singing backup and occasional lead vocals. Jones was complimented by two female singers, Jenny Soule and Gloria "Granola" who were needed to add authenticity to Steely Dan's next single 'My Old School' (the studio version of which featured top session singers Myrna and Shirley Mathews and Vanetta Fields).

Along with all the success Steely Dan achieved in 1973 was a fair amount of criticism. Rolling Stone's James Isaacs felt that too often they came off as a "limp dildo". While top-rated New York disc-jockey Dan Ingram quipped, "Steely Dan? Another piece of crap for the people who love it," during an

---

centered almost exclusively around this new Palmer sound, in the end it was determined that Fagen's distinct vocals had already been established as something of a Steely Dan trademark and it would be futile to try to replace him. Palmer would be given a second chance with ABC Records in 1978 with his band Wa-koo aka The Big Wa-koo.

The Grateful Dead of Beverly Boulevard

interview with the Long Island based Newsday[31].

Like many rock bands of this period, Steely Dan's appearance was hippie-esque. Their concert performances were erratic and with David Palmer as their frontman- the early public version of Steely Dan was really well…..bogus. Early supporter, David Proctor, noted after a January 1973 concert that "Steely Dan abandoned, almost totally, the mutli-rythmic base that punctuated their outstanding first album", at their debut Salt Lake City concert-sharing a bill incidentally with the Doobie Brothers.[32]

With Fagen's distinctive quasi-Northeast vocals holding together their two hit singles it made no sense to trot out Palmer and foister him off as the "voice" of Steely Dan in concert. Perhaps the best take on Palmer's presence in the Steely Dan camp came from the Village Voice's Robert Christgau when he quipped that Palmer, "fit in like a cheerleader at a crap game[33]."

---

[31] Newsday April 12, 1973

[32] Salt Lake City Tribune 1/29/73 p.9 Proctor also stated "I can't figure out why they would drop the great songs they have done already for newer, less asthetic stuff...Showmanship. I guess."

[33] Village Voice July 1973

The Steely Dan File

Essentially Palmer's days were numbered once 'Do It Again' hit the charts in November of 1972 and over by the time 'Reeling In The Years' went Top 20 in April of 1973. After a concert in California Palmer was officially asked to leave the band. Palmer's time with Steely Dan was a rare episode of the band's leaders miscalculating someone's talent and purpose to the Steely Dan sound. Palmer had a good voice and was talented[34] but he was a mismatch for Steely Dan and the sooner out of the way the better.

Continuing with the "singles and touring" formula at the behest of tour manager Joel Cohen, during the latter part of 1973 the now five piece Steely Dan[35] became restless. 'My Old School', the new single, bombed much like 'Show Biz Kids', despite a second appearance on both American Bandstand and the Midnight Special to promote it. The end of 1973 saw the 'Dan reeling from the sophomore jinx and retiring into the re-

---

[34] News Record (Vermont) 4/28/78 p.54- Palmer wrote much of the material for the band Wha-Koo, a pop-rock band that issued 2 lp's in the late '70's.

[35] For the Countdown To Ecstasty tour Steely Dan actually increased to eight with Royce Jones, Jenny Soule and Gloria Granola added as back up singers.

The Grateful Dead of Beverly Boulevard

cording studio to work on their third album at the Village Recorder in West Hollywood.

Rock n Roll with Class

Seven short months after the release of their commercially disappointing second album, Steely Dan were back with the eleven track Pretzel Logic, a tour de force musically that would also become their biggest seller to date, climbing to the #8 spot on the Billboard album chart. Completed with a number of session players like Jim Gordon (drums), Dean Parks (guitar) and Tim Schmit (vocals), the album incorporated diverse musical styles from folk rock ('With A Gun') to jazz ('East St. Louis Toddle-oo') and also contained a Top 40 favorite in the short, catchy track 'Rikki Don't Lose That Number'. It received a slew of rave reviews upon its' release in March of 1974[36].

Perhaps the quickest Steely Dan album ever recorded *Pretzel Logic* was a hodgepodge of old and new compositions. Included among the recordings was the only cover version the band would ever record, the 1927 Duke Ellington theme 'East St.Louis Toodle- oo', a snappy number and perhaps the most unlikely song one would ever hear on a "rock" record of this era. Steely Dan's

---

[36] The New York weekly, The Village Voice gave 'Logic and A+ rating and felt that Fagen's vocals, "seem like the golden mean of technique". March 18, 1974

version of the Ellington song was remarkably faithful to the original 1927 version and Fagen was rightly proud of it, even having a specially pressed promo version of it sent to the aging jazz legend. "It was Duke's birthday recently, and I sent him a copy of the record,' Fagen told Britain's Melody Maker, "I would have been very flattered if he had heard it."[37]

It is not known if Ellington ever heard the modern version of 'East St. Louis Toodle-oo' , as he passed away a short time after the recording was issued, but it was apparent at this early stage in their careers that Fagen and Becker were big time jazz fans. One of their early compositions, 'Parker's Band', was recorded for 'Logic and was transformed into a unique "bop-rock" track to launch side two of the album. Jazz great Plas Johnson played sax on the speedy two minute ode to the be-bop great Charlie Parker and marked the continuing trend of bringing in classy jazz players to play on Steely Dan lp's.

Percussionist Victor Feldman returned yet again to Steely Dan's recording sessions and added his distinct effect to the albums' opening track, the soon to be classic 'Rikki,

---

[37] Melody Maker June 1974

The Grateful Dead of Beverly Boulevard

Don't Lose That Number'. That's Feldman playing the odd flopanda at the songs quiet opening and the song of course was controversial among the jazz crowd as it borrowed the riff that made up the Bluenote classic 'Song For My Father' by Horace Silver.

John Coltrane was another Steely Dan favorite, although Fagen saw his free form style as the basis for the ponderous fusion that filled the airwaves of the early 1970's, "John Coltrane was a fantastic player" Fagen commented to Melody Maker's Chris Welch, "But he was responsible for leading people into making a terrible mistake. I preferred John before his modal period when he was with the Miles Davis Quintet." Although, also a big fan of Miles, Fagen felt that in the fusion era Davis had "gone over the edge"[38].

All influences considered, and there were many non-jazz influences on *Pretzel Logic*, and Fagen did not want to portray Steely Dan as outside of the rock 'n roll circle. "I like to think that we are a rock and roll band…..with class."[39] Fagen declared, and although he noted that he and Becker were the sole composers for the band, "the solos and arrangements come from the group. There is room for improvisation."

---

[38] Melody Maker June 24, 1974, "Melody Maker Band Break Down:Steely Dan" by Chris Welch
[39] LA Times March 1974

The Steely Dan File

The impact of *Pretzel Logic* was important on several levels for Steely Dan- it restored them both sales-wise and reputation-wise. For one fleeting moment in 1974 Steely Dan was even viewed as the top, hip "California" band around. They were dubbed by no-less than Byrd biographer Bud Scoppa as "one of the best...most original" American rock groups. Scoppa also found their music "accessible and sophisticated" in a glowing article in the counter-culture bible of the day *Rolling Stone*.[40]

It was through Gary Katz that Steely Dan was able to make a deep California connection by supporting Thomas Jefferson Kaye, aka Tommy Kaye, on his second solo album in 1974. The ABC Dunhill release *First Grade* was produced by Katz, and featured contributions from Fagen, Becker and Baxter. A highlight of this psychedelic-folk opus is the Fagen/Becker track 'American Lovers, which critic Robert Christgau labeled a, "bitter, poignant farewell to the counterculture,[41]" *First*

---

[40] Rolling Stone 5/23/74 p.73 "Stainless Steely Band" by Bud Scoppa. Scoppa authored the first Byrds biography in 1971

[41] Dean of American Rock Critics website http://www.robertchristgau.com/get_artist.php?id=1578&name=Thomas+Jefferson+Kaye

The Grateful Dead of Beverly Boulevard

Grade seems to represent a swansong for the entire California folk rock era. For Steely Dan aficionados it serves as a link from their earliest days in California (i.e. The 'Dallas' sessions) to the present (ie.The *Pretzel Logic* sessions) and would be a farewell to their unique New York meets LA country-rock sound.

Sales-wise *Pretzel Logic* was a winner and its success would ensure Fagen and Becker a little more leeway when it came to dealing with record company execs and business managers. '*Logic* climbed to #8 on the Billboard and outsold it's two predecessors, spending 19 weeks in the Top 40. The single 'Rikki Don't Lose That Number' meanwhile was a monster hit, topping the US chart in many regions, spending 11 weeks on Billboard's Top 40 pop chart.

Coinciding with the release of *Pretzel Logic* was the last major tour undertaken by the original Steely Dan ensemble. Added to the touring band was drummer Jeff Porcaro and keyboardist/vocalist Mike McDonald; while remaining from the previous tour was vocalist/percussionist Royce Jones. The original five: Becker, Dias, Baxter, Fagen and Hodder now had three albums under their belt and were coming into their own in concert. The tour opened April 3, 1974 in New

The Steely Dan File

York after a series of warm-up gigs in Los Angeles and Southern California[42].

Several high quality bootleg recordings exist from the 1974 Steely Dan tour that show the band to be spirited, if erratic performers. Their emcee Jerome Aniton was often drunk when introducing them. Their leader Donald Fagen was both an extrovert and introvert; bouncing around conducting one moment, relegating lead vocals to his back-up singer the next[43] And their two guitarist Baxter and Dias clashed amid styles ranging from Jimi Hendrix to Billy Bauer. But like their albums Steely Dan gave the customer his moneys worth. An added bonus on the 1974 tour was the performance of an unreleased track called, 'Mobile Home', which was performed at the conclusion of every

---

[42] The Valley news (Van Nuys) 3/8/74-'Steely Dan Returning to Glendale' by Vic Field Steely Dan was very much the house band of the small Glendale nightclub 'The Ice House' later re-named 'Sopwith Camel Club', after a fire. They played four warm up concerts their in early March of 1974.

[43] Fagen in fact does not even sing lead vocals on the only official live recording ever released by the original Steely Dan, 'Bodhissatva', which was issued on a 45 in 1980. Fagen's conducting of the band brought him to be compared to Frank Zappa, whose Mothers of Invention also had a large entourage that included two drummers as Steely Dan's 1974 band did.

The Grateful Dead of Beverly Boulevard

concert. This track was never included on any Steely Dan album.

After six weeks of coast-to-coast concerts in the U.S. the 'Dan took off for England where an enthusiastic following was waiting. In the UK Steely Dan played some of their best live music. Melody Maker's Chris Welch called their opening concert in Manchester a "sensational set" and his high regard for them brought them to be compared to none other than the Beatles: "Rikki Don't' Lose That Number is pure pop, the three minute song given its highest status since the days of the Beatles...Steely Dan will open a few ears to the way rock can be moved forward without losing its' roots, who knows in time maybe we can love them as well." In England at least Steely Dan were recognized for the enormous talent they were, but the American rock press was catching up.

Billboard Magazine, always one of Steely Dan's biggest supporters, named them as "one of the groups that has managed to save rock from the complete doldrums"[44] The Village Voice's Robert Christgau called the early Steely Dan sound, "perfect licks that crackle and buzz when you

---

[44] 'Spotlight' Billboard April 2,1975

The Steely Dan File

listen hard, Grass Roots harmonies applied to words that are usually twisted.[45]"

Even Rolling Stone magazine, originally cool to the band, had come around to see the 'Dan's unique perspective of rock music. Charles Perry was sent to track down the group for their sole cover feature[46] and his "Steely Dan Comes Up Swinging- #5 ...with a dildo" was an extensive profile that secured their "cult" following with the uninhibited embrace that Steely Dan was "America's unlikeliest supergroup".

Throughout the tour however friction had been increasing among the original five Steely Dan members. Jeff Baxter, who had received enthusiastic praise for his guitar playing throughout much of the tour, wanted the band to keep performing live throughout the summer despite the fact that Steely Dan had no more scheduled concerts after their July 5th concert in Santa Monica, California.

Originally it seemed Becker and Fagen had no problems with the freelancing of Steely Dan's members to other bands. When the Doobie Brothers, whom Steely Dan had been touring with, offered Baxter a chance to

---

[45]Village Voice, July 15,1973
[46]Rolling Stone 8/15/1974

The Grateful Dead of Beverly Boulevard

guest on their world tour he readily agreed and was soon on his way back to London for a major concert[47]. Jim Hodder, the original drummer whose role may have been cramped a bit with the arrival of Jeff Porcaro et al, also wanted to continue touring. In a show of rare rock family camaraderie Hodder and Dias even lent their talent and performed as backing musicians for Linda Rondstadt during some shows in the late summer of '74.

In early August matters came to a head with the exiting of both Baxter and Hodder from the band. Baxter immediately became a permanent Doobie Brother and would enjoy much of the fruits of their late 1970's success[48]. Jim Hodder meanwhile headed north and started his own band in the San Fran-

---

[47]Baxter also played concerts with Elton John during this period and was officially told of his dismissal from Steely Dan via a phone call from LA to London.

[48]Baxter's joining to the ranks of the Warner Brothers signed Doobie Brothers, and the subsequent addition of Michael McDonald (another member of the 1974 Steely Dan) led to specualtion that Fagen and Becker themselves had already inked a deal with Warner Brothers by late 1974 and that this transfering of members to the label was only a prelude to a 1977 Steely Dan Warner Brothers album. Becker and Fagen themselves would not admit to any affiliation with Warner until interviews in 1977 when they thought their contract with ABC Records might be terminated.

The Steely Dan File

cisco area, stating in a 1977 interview[49] that he was living nicely off the royalties from *Can't Buy A Thrill*.[50]

With the official break-up of the original band Fagen and Becker told ABC Records[51] and their manager Joel Cohen that they would have to shelve their plans for an autumn tour. Like a comet the original Steely Dan vanished from the hoopla of the rock world, never to perform live again.

Halfway Crucified

As the dust settled from the collapse of the original Steely Dan ensemble Donald

---

[49] "Steely Dan's Golden Aja" New Times October 1977

[50] Hodder's post Steely Dan work included sessions with Sammy Hagar and David Soul. Hodder would die tragically by drowning at his home in Marin Country, California in 1991.

[51] ABC Records had phased out their one time moniker of ABC Dunhill Records in 1973. Dunhill had itself been a separate label in the mid-1960's, founded by impressario Lou Adler. Before it's merger in 1979 with MCA Records ABC was accused of many irregularities regarding the payment of royalties in a major lawsuit brought by former Mommas & Poppa's leader John Phillips in 1977. Fagen and Becker themselves accused the label of non-payement and tried legal action the rid them of their 1972 contract to no avail.

The Grateful Dead of Beverly Boulevard

Fagen and Walter Becker would be in a unique position for mid-1970's rock stars. Freed from the trappings of the annually nationwide tour to promote each new album Fagen and Becker, along with producer Katz and engineer Nichols would create a "floating workshop" version of Steely Dan that would result in perhaps the best pop music of the decade.

Not that they hadn't created a few enemies in their retreat from the world of mainstream rock. Joel Cohen, their tour manager, for one was not happy, slapping Fagen and Becker with a breach of contract lawsuit that was eventually settled out of court. ABC Records themselves were not pleased with the fact that Steely Dan would not be performing live in 1975 and put pressure on the songwriters to come up quickly with the remaining albums required in Steely Dan's 1972 contract.[52]

---

[52] Cohen was also the manager of fellow ABC act Three Dog Night and authored a colorful book about their exploits ('Three Dog Night and Me"). Cohen's personnel agencency, Kudo III, is listed in the credits on the *Pretzel Logic* but his relationship with Steely Dan was always strained at best. Steely Dan's contract with ABC called for 8 albums and initially expired in 1976. Subsequentally Fagen and Becker announced that they had signed with Warner Brothers soon after.

The Steely Dan File

To Fagen and Becker the *Pretzel Logic* tour had left them "penniless, infirm and disillusioned" and that it was better to part ways with the band members that wanted to continue to tour "until our very dicks turned green and fell off.[53]" Exit Baxter and Hodder. And Cohen. Steely Dan II was forming…

By mid-1975 Steely Dan had scored 3 gold albums, 4 Top 40 hit singles and more importantly a loyal following of fans and critics. FM radio, responsible for their first break-through in 1972, held them up as gods and would make them the backbone of the Album Oriented Rock radio format as the decade progressed.

In the second half of the 1970's Fagen and Becker would transform from leaders of a popular, off-beat looking pop rock band into enigmatic Los Angeles anti-heroes….mainly by doing…. nothing…..Steely Dan would essentially disappear from the rock world…..record what they wanted….when they wanted….dabble in jazz…blow off the Grammy's…move back to New York….and break up.

---

[53] Liner notes to the remastered edition of *Katy Lied*, MCA 1999

The Grateful Dead of Beverly Boulevard

Steely Dan 1974 Releases
Pretzel Logic (March 1974)
Despite keeping the original lineup for their concerts Pretzel Logic would in fact be the first Steely Dan album recorded under their "floating workshop" format. Walter Becker would make his Steely Dan debut on guitar ('With A Gun'), Donald Fagen would play his only notes as a saxophonist ('East St. Louis toodle-oo') and session legend Jim Gordon would be installed as the band's drummer for the entire album. The result was somewhat erratic, but still very enjoyable.

Rating   1 2 3 4 5 6 7 **8** 9 10

The Steely Dan File

- **Rikki Don't Lose That Number/ Any Major Dude (April 1974)**

With the release and quick success of 'Rikki Don't Lose That Number' (it hit #4 on the Billboard Top 40) Fagen and Becker permanently established themselves as two of the premiere composers of contemporary American pop music. 'Rikki' was perhaps one of the most perfect singles of the decade and alongside its' predecessors 'Do It Again' and "Reeling In The Years' stands as a trophy to the early Steely Dan ensemble. Perhaps erratic in concert (but who wasn't in those days) the early '70's Steely Dan were masters in the recording studio. Ultimate trivia: Back up vocals on 'Rikki' were done by none other than Timothy B. Schmitt, future Eagles lead vocalist.

- **Pretzel Logic/ Through With Buzz (September 1974)**

A minor hit single when issued in 1974 'Pretzel Logic' would eventually be the track that brought Steely Dan back to life in the early 1990's. When issued as a live recording (with Mike McDonald on back up vocals) 'Logic would hit #17 on Billboard's Rock Tracks chart in 1991 and put Steely Dan back on the map in rock circles.

2
The Floating Workshop

1975-1981

The Steely Dan File

The Floating Workshop

Thanks to still being in the good graces of ABC President ("and absolute ruler") Jay Lasker, the now road weary and jaded Steely Dan still had a recording contract *and* a budget despite collapsing Steely Dan I in August of 1974. Retiring to their small office at ABC/Dunhill Records Fagen and Becker set out to "begin work on a new suite of songs which would someday adorn the greatest Steely Dan album ever."[54]

---

[54] Liner notes to *Katy Lied* remastered edition MCA/Victor c.1999

The Steely Dan File

Confident and secure in the studio Fagen and Becker delved into new recording sessions in Los Angeles and in early 1975 emerged with what they hoped would be the recording milestone of the decade in the 10 track epic *Katy Lied*.

Something happened on the way to the temple however and when the master tapes for the new album were permanently marred by a faulty noise reduction system at ABC Records recording studios Fagen and Becker contemplated scrapping the album altogether.

After much fiddling with the knobs however a decent master was conjured up and forwarded to ABC Records for release in March of 1975. The scenario however had now left the two parties with virtually no lines of communication. As a result, sales for *Katy Lied* were lackluster and despite a great lead single ('Black Friday') it peaked at only #13 on the US charts.

As the summer of 1975 progressed the 'Dan was morphing into what Gary Katz would term a "floating workshop"[55]. After the '*Katy Lied*' sessions ended both Jeff Porcaro and Mike McDonald would officially leave the Steely Dan ensemble thus terminating

---

[55] Musician, Player & Listener, Jan.1979

The Floating Workshop

the band remnant from the 1974 tour. Only Denny Dias now remained from both the original *Can't Buy A Thrill* band as well as the 1974-touring ensemble. Porcaro, who played on 9 of the 10 songs on *Katy Lied*, would soon emerge with his own pop supergroup in Toto. He would reappear at Steely Dan sessions throughout the rest of the decade but never appear on as many tracks of the 'Dan as he did in the mid-'70's.s

Mike McDonald meanwhile, Fagen's main back-up singer from 1973-1975, would essentially replace lead singer Tom Johnston in the Doobie Brothers and bring the band to great heights with a series of soul pop classics in the late 1970's. His Steely Dan work in the late '70's was limited in quantity by not quality and his distinct vocals on tracks like 'Rose Darling', 'Kid Charlemagne' and 'Peg' made those songs shine.

Top-notch jazz players for the *Katy Lied* sessions included some big names. Drum legend Hal Blaine was brought in to master a re-working of the 1973 track 'Any World'. Jazz Crusaders Wilton Felder and Larry Carlton played on several tracks and for Carlton it marked the beginning of a deep and important musical alliance. Percussionist Victor Feldman returned yet again, to add some

The Steely Dan File

perfect sounds to a new version of the 1972 track 'Everyone's Gone to the Movies' and bop heir Phil Woods added a perfect sax solo to the elegant 'Dr. Wu'. Additional guitar work came from New York session man Hugh McCracken as well as Becker's old pal Rick Derringer, who returned with a dazzling solo on 'Chain Lightnin'.

Two other stalwarts of Steely Dan's 1974/5 floating workshop included bassist Chuck Rainey and pianist Michael Omartian. In some ways Omartian's sound gave *Katy Lied* a sophisticated grace to it- the album even ends with an almost Bill Evans-like flurrie that Omartian apparently made up on the spot. Rainey was an extraordinary talent who would essentially replace Becker as the Steely Dan bass player for the rest of the decade. His contributions to the Steely Dan sound in the years ahead would be considerable and mighty.

Despite all this help Fagen and Becker still considered *Katy Lied* a disappointment, the one that got away. When the album was finally released in the spring of 1975 it was warmly received by some in music press.
Long champions of Becker & Fagen, Billboard Magazine led the charge of the believers,

The Floating Workshop

claiming Steely Dan was "certainly the premiere American rock band to emerge in several years" and "there is great skill in making complicated music sound easy, and this is exactly what Steely Dan does time after time."[56]   Citing what they termed as Steely Dan's "mammoth following" Billboard predicted a big hit with the album.

By June it appeared that Billboard was right on the mark; the LP had shot into the U.S. Top 20 and the lead single 'Black Friday' was climbing into the Top 40. The unproductive relationship between Steely Dan and ABC records, however would undermine Katy Lied's sales. Aside from a full-page ad in trade publications ABC's publicity department did nothing to promote Steely Dan in 1975.

As a result, the next single 'Bad Sneakers' became the first Steely Dan single to not make Billboard's Hot 100 since the limited release of 'Dallas'/'Sail The Waterway' in early 1972. Fagen and Becker didn't help matters by giving no interviews throughout the year and refusing to perform even a limited number of dates. They were a popular act but the idea of being one of the important "super" groups now held little appeal to them.

---

[56] Billboard 4/5/75 Album Spotlight

The Steely Dan File

Across the Atlantic Steely Dan did score another Top 40 hit in 1975 when 'Do It Again' from the first album hit #37 on the U.K. chart. Katy Lied was also moderately popular in Britain and became their biggest seller to date there, hitting #13 in July.

Steely Dan 1975 Releases
Katy Lied (April 1975)

The first Steely Dan album that was not promoted with a tour Katy Lied was received with mixed reviews upon release in the spring of 1975. Not a challenging set for the listener it was a great combination of old and new visions of the Steely Dan world. 'Black Friday' was a bouncy tale of an impending stock market crash, punctuated perfectly by Becker's funky guitar solo. Doctor Wu a beautiful ode to drug induced melancholia, while 'Everyone's Gone To The Movies' was a rewind to dodgy imagery of Can't Buy A Thrill, the album the song was originally intended for. The remaining members of the 1974 touring ensemble, namely Becker, Fagen, Dias, Porcaro and McDonald served as the core band for many of the recording sessions and were supplemented by the likes of Feldman, Rainey, Felder, Derringer and sax legend Phil Woods. FM radio loved Katy Lied, while the 'Dan's bubblegum crowd began to drift. Album sales were moderate and sales of the lp's two singles failed to generate any Top 10 hits.

Rating 1 2 3 4 5 6 7 **8** 9 10

The Floating Workshop

- **Black Friday/ Throw Back The Little Ones** (April 1975)

Had Steely Dan toured to promote it, 'Black Friday' would have been their 4th Top 20 hit single. With no publicity at all it was left to drift up to #37 and fade away quickly. A funky little Fagen R&B number, 'Black Friday' suffers a bit in the mix-the bass is too low and the keyboards seem to disappear after a nifty intro. The song is held together with rapid-fire vocals from Fagen, great high harmonies from McDonald and awesome axe work from new lead guitar man Becker. Porcaro's drums are excellent as usual. The flip side is one of those definitive Steely Dan New York numbers- Brooklyn meets upstate with a horn section that emulates Zappa very well.

- **Bad Sneakers/ Chain Lightnin'** (August 1975)

The biggest bomb of Steely Dan's chart history to date, 'Bad Sneakers' is an ode to the lonely wandering Steely Dan-this time in midtown near Radio City. The flip side is cool 'Dan noire- supposedly about a Nazi rally. Wicked Derringer solo to boot.

The Steely Dan File

Some Babies grow In a Peculiar Way

When 1976 dawned Fagen and Becker stood as an oddity in the US rock scene. With the lukewarm success of *Katy Lied* and the growing success of the large number of ex-Steely Dan members[57], they could be excused for feeling a little irrelevant at the dawn of the Carter Administration.

In a year where the number one album was a sonically buoyant live album (*Frampton Comes Alive* by ex-Humble Pie guitarist Peter Frampton) Steely Dan were positively invisible. In an era marked by glam power pop (Kiss) and arena rock (Styx et al) Steely Dan

---

[57] Not only were the new members of the Doobie Brothers riding high, but even the lightweight David Palmer had proven his meddle by penning a Gold single with Carole King, 'Jazz Man', a US #1 in late 1974.

The Floating Workshop

were serving up pop literature, influenced by Burroughs, Kerouac and Vonnegut. Their mid-70's output could have been marketed along with a short story paperback, for it was appealing to a sense of intellect foreign to the rock world Rather than turn into a super-group Steely Dan had turned into an invisible group with a well known name and a moderately large cult following, numbering about 500,000.

Katy Lied and it's following up *The Royal Scam* both sold a little over 500,000 copies in their initial run, hardly mega-hits in an era of mega-sellers like *Songs In The Key of Life* by Stevie Wonder (a double album. that *debuted* at #1 upon it's release in 1976), *Their Greatest Hits-* an early Eagles compilation released in 1975 (now with some 27 million copies sold) and anything from Fleetwood Mac released during this period.

Steely Dan- the big important, next big thing had fallen off the radar and had become almost non-existent by the time Fagen and Becker went back into the studios to record *The Royal Scam* in the late summer of '75.

After a series of taxing sessions in New York, Steely Dan (now essentially just Fagen

The Steely Dan File

[vocals, keyboards] and Becker [guitar, occasional bass]) returned to Los Angeles and completed the album in early 1976.

Using more horns than on previous albums Steely Dan brought in arranger Gary Sherman to give some of the record an overtly commercial sound, commercial as in "you're watching the ABC Records television network (the ending of 'Sign In Stranger') or commercial as in early smooth jazz (John Klemmer on 'Caves of Altamira'). (bass), Paul Griffin (keyboards) and Bernard Purdie (drums). Fagen's vocals were good-not hidden, not obvious. The guitar work was the album's real power and *The Royal Scam* featured incredibly licks from Becker, Elliot Randall, Dias and significantly Larry Carlton, who assisted Fagen and Becker by preparing

The lyrics were more obvious, the sound funky LA pop (thanks to a rhythm section consisting of Chuck Rainey rhythm charts for the sessions. The brassy horns were put together by session great Jim Horn, Slyde Hyde and ex-Tijuana Brass members Chuck and Bob Findley.

All in all it was the most complete Steely Dan album since *Countdown To Ecstasy*, in no small part to the production/engineering

The Floating Workshop

axis of Katz and Nichols. Like *Countdown* however, *'Royal Scam* presented itself as a marketing nightmare for ABC Records[58].

Now headed by new "nice" president Steve Diener (he would write some of the rather overblown liner notes to original vinyl edition of *Aja*), ABC Records was a record company on the way down in the mid-70's. Faced with a lawsuit that suggested faulty bookkeeping practices by former Momma's and the Poppa's leader John Phillips, the label was still clinging to Three Dog Night as their top band in 1976.

With the *Royal Scam* ABC felt that they had no obvious single to promote the album with- the album was a sort of American version of progressive rock- great for FM, not so great for Top 40 radio. In the words of the magazine Hit Parade Steely Dan had become "America's answer to Procul Harum"[59].

---

[58] Perhaps with help from ABC's publicity department Fagen and Becker appeared on the cover of the pop magazine Cashbox in June of 1976, in front of a jukebox, hinting at their hit single songwriting ability.

[59] Hit Parader, August 1976

The Steely Dan File

Other acts still on ABC in 1976 included Tom Petty, Jimmy Buffett, Stephen Bishop and Chaka Kahn. With their well-known name ABC Records put a lot of money that Steely Dan could get back into the Top 10 and score a few hit singles as they had done in their previous incarnation in 1972-74. They were about a year off.

Although 'Kid Charlemagne' was a bouncy, even disco influenced, opening track from '*The Royal Scam*, it did not really lend itself to AM radio 1976, which Stevie Wonder aside, was perhaps the dullest year for Top 40 radio in the entire decade. Fagen and Becker themselves were pretty much out of the loop as far as how to market Steely Dan by this point, even appearing on the cover on the pop chart magazine Cashbox to plug the album's release. 'Charlemagne however was no 'Do It Again'(#6), it wasn't even a 'Pretzel Logic'(#57)- having peaked at #82 on Billboard's Hot 100 it failed to even chart in Cashbox, keeping sales of the parent album from taking off into multi-platinum status as the bicentennial summer progressed.

Desperate for any kind of "hit" for Steely Dan in 1976 ABC Records pushed for 'The Fez' to be issued in September of 1976.

The Floating Workshop

Although a cool and funky atmospheric track, 'The Fez' was not AM radio fodder either (it's very doubtful that any major market AM station even played it) and in a different time would have been perfect as dance remix track for Studio 54. In any event by the fall of 1976 Steely Dan had very little chart presence in the US and virtually no presence in the rock world.

The nine track *The Royal Scam LP* had emerged in late May of 1976 and was a virtual carbon copy of *Katy Lied* chart wise, reaching #15 in June . Again the album tended to be enjoyed more by the FM audience than the AM Top 40 crowd. Heavy on production, darker, more lyrically enigmatic, *The Royal Scam* was a break from the past for Fagen and Becker as it took them back to New York for the first time in almost six years. Many of the songs seemed like mini-novels, coded inferences to be deduced by shrewd listeners. Who was 'Kid Charlemagne'? What was 'The Fez'? Where was "Mizar 5"? As critic Ken Tucker put it in his Rolling Stone review[60], "Their latest album, The Royal Scam, is their most atypical re-

---

[60] Rolling Stone 5/76

The Steely Dan File

cord, possessing neither obvious AM material nor seductive lyrical mysteriousness ."

Although they again failed to put together a touring band to promote The Royal Scam Fagen and Becker did consent to a few lengthy interviews. Flying to London to plug the albums release there, the trio of Becker, Fagen and Katz engaged in a detailed discussion with Melody Maker. Back in the states they talked to The Music Gig (December 1976), New Times (June 1976) and Newsweek (August 23,1976).

In these interviews they seemed to hint that they might tour once again in the coming year. In fact The Music Gig titled one of their pieces "Steely Dan Hits The Road" (May 1977) and Rolling Stone announced in their Random Notes column that Steely Dan's first tour in three years would begin sometime in 1977. Unfortunately it all ended up being wishful thinking.

With a studio ensemble that relied heavily on high salaried session players the cost of putting the new Steely Dan on stage was daunting. Players brought in on the 1975-1976 sessions included drummer Bernard Purdie, sax man John Klemmer, bassist Chuck Rainey and dazzling guitar heroes

The Floating Workshop

Larry Carlton and Elliot Randall. Becker himself now figured prominently in Steely Dan's guitar sound, while Fagen received keyboard help from Paul Griffin and continued support from the perennial Victor Feldman. Future Eagle member Tim Schmit was brought in to help Fagen with backing vocals as was the - now permanent Doobie Brother- Mike McDonald who'd officially left the Steely Dan camp in 1975.

Participating less and less at the Steely Dan recording sessions and soon himself to be officially out of the band was original band member Denny Dias. Dias was a close confidant of both Fagen and Becker and had settled nicely into LA with his family. After cutting his final solo with the band (on a track called 'Beyond The Seawall'[61]) Dias left Steely Dan and joined jazz great Hampton Hawes[62] ensemble in 1976. When Hawes

---

[61] 'Beyond the Seawall' was incorporated into the song 'Aja' and marked Dias' last appearance on an album for two decades. He next appeared on Dave Garfield's 'Tribute To Jeff Porcaro' in 1996.

[62] Hawes was another underrated hero from the bop era, a pianist of considerable talent he had his career disrupted by a pot bust in the late '50's. He was later

The Steely Dan File

passed away in 1977 Dias all but retired from the music world and would only appear on a recording again twenty years later on a tribute album to the late drummer Jeff Porcaro.

Although the *Royal Scam* failed to spawn a Top 40 hit in the US, 1976 did end on an up note for Steely Dan overseas with a Top 20 UK hit single in 'Haitian Divorce'. Culled from side two of *The Royal Scam* the six minute 'Divorce had quirky reggae/Latin sound and distinctive percussive flair and became Steely Dan's biggest European hit peaking at #17 in Britain while charting briefly in Belgium and Spain.

Overseas would provide the songwriters with vivid lyrical and musical inspiration in the year ahead and their unique ability to appeal to the hip and not so hip would culminate in a remarkable period of LP and singles successes. Steely Dan was about to enter their golden age with an album that invoked

---

pardoned by President John F. Kennedy and released from prison in 1962. Dias made one album with Hawes, a live set recorded at Half Moon Bay, California.

The Floating Workshop

imagery over a girl Fagen called "Korean Colleen"[63]

1976 Steely Dan Releases

- **Kid Charlemagne/Green Earrings(ABC Records) (May 1976)-**

In so many ways one of the best singles ever issued by the 'Dan, this record inexplicably bombed big time on the US charts. Peaking at #82 in Billboard, 'Charlemagne even failed to break onto Cashbox's single chart. Possibly had Green Earrings been the A-side it would have done better. Both tracks were funkier than previous 'Dan singles and both included insanely perfect guitar solos. Larry Carlton gives us the wicked slick LA sound on Kid; Elliot Randall and Denny Dias bring up the funk on Earrings.

---

[63] Radio interview KPKA, Santa Monica, Fagen claimed that there was a real girl with the name *Ajia* and that she was the bride of a neighbor who'd served in the Korean War.

The Steely Dan File

The Royal Scam (May 1976)

Seen by many listeners at the time as a concept album, The Royal Scam was in some ways Steely Dan's most literate album. Listening to it all the way through literally brought the listener to another world…in this case a world of drug enthusiasts, hostage takers, jewel thieves and Puerto Rican immigrants. The lyrics were wonderfully deep, comical and sometimes profound. 'Sign In Stranger' sounded like a Mafia recruitment campaign from another planet, 'Caves of Altamira' as if it was sonically recorded in those historical monuments. 'Scam was the boys attempt to take on all of the artsy-fartsy posturing of the then hallowed world of prog-rock and for a time brought them in to comparison with Procol Harum. The rhythms are funky, the jazz-classic Fagen fake jazz and the guitar solos….well there's a reason they were called STEELy Dan!

Rating 1 2 3 4 5 6 7 8 **9** 10

- **The Fez/ Sign In Stranger (Sept. 1976)**
  A minor hit single, The Fez now marked 5 consecutive singles that failed to break the US Top 10 since the summer '74 success of 'Rikki'. Had the boys lost their touch? Hardly, they were just ahead of their time; Fez would have been a perfect song to remix for the heyday of 12' singles that was just around the corner. Sign In Stranger was sort of an early new wave track…odd lyrics, Feldman piano, fuzzy guitar, tv theme show ending….cool.

The Floating Workshop

The Land of Steely Dan

By the fall of 1976 Donald Fagen and Walter Becker had secured their place in the 1970's rock scene as the coolest and smartest personas of the time. Despite their difficult relationship with both the media and their record company they still seemed to be calling most of the shots. Their records stretched the boundaries of what pop music had been in a way similar to the Beatles, yet emanated from a myriad of influences from Tin Pan Alley, the Gershwins to be-bop. Their horn arrangements sometimes sounded like TV commercials, their lyrics remained cryptic sometimes, obvious the other.

With 1977 upon them they were able to visualize their Steely Dan creation into the amalgam of all that was going on in pop mu-

The Steely Dan File

sic in the late '70's. From smooth jazz to disco funkiness, from trippy Asiatic visions to high-class Manhattan socialites the land of Steely Dan was a feast for the ears and a trip for the mind.

Work on their new album began in late 1976 and was originally planned to have been a double album[64] and to have coincided with a US tour. Its working title was *Ajia* and was at one time to include a song about Napoleon and another called 'Were You Blind That Day'[65]. Exceptional jazz players were brought in to compliment Steely Dan regulars Chuck Rainey, Victor Feldman and Larry Carlton. Joe Sample from the Crusaders (electric piano), Wayne Shorter of Weather Report (tenor sax) and session masters like Tom Scott (sax) and Ernie Watts

---

[64] Music Gig "Steely Dan Hit The Road" May 1977. Article contains an interview with sax player and arranger Tom Scott. Fagen and Becker were hoping that if they issued a 2 record set that it would free them from their record contract at ABC Records.

[65] New Times 10/29/77 "Steely Dan's Golden Aja". Fagen mentions that 5 songs have been completed, including the two mentioned. The "Napolean song" appears to have been scrapped, "Were You Blind That Day" is thought to have been re-written as the track "Third World Man".

The Floating Workshop

(sax) all contributed to the bright new sound of Steely Dan[66].

With all the right people in place Steely Dan's sixth album, *Aja* (pronounced "asia"), was recognized as a true masterpiece in the history of pop and rock music almost immediately upon release. Reviewers were tripping over themselves looking for superlatives to describe it, while record buyers couldn't get enough of it. Hitting the stores in early October of 1977 it would be certified Gold (for 500,000 copies sold) within days and begin getting extensive airplay on every major radio station in the country, regardless of whether the station was Album Oriented Rock, Top 40 or even disco. It was an exciting new sound. From the opening notes of soft funk on 'Black Cow' the new Steely Dan style was evident. Becker called it "sound sculpture"[67] and admitted that he even listened to KC and the Sunshine Band when not listening to Monk and Bird et al. Hard core rock purists, led by the UK publication Hit

---

[66] Fagen called it a "stylistic change", New Times 10/29/77

[67] New York Times 10/9/77 "America's Best Maybe Rock Non-band" by Robert Palmer

The Steely Dan File

Parader and underground rag Creem, saw it as a disco sellout, but on the whole it was the best received 'Dan album ever. As critic Cameron Crowe put it, "against all odds it was Steely Dan fever"[68].

1977 Steely Dan Releases

Aja (October 1977)

When Aja was issued in the autumn of 1977 the great war between rock and disco was raging. Any group that dared to stray off the rock formula radar was a traitor or worse. Since they had receded from the rock arena to the point of invisibility by 1977 Steely Dan were to many critics the personification of all that was wrong in the rock world. But Aja

---

[68] Crowe did a large article on Steely Dan in the year ending issue of Rolling Stone in 1977 and wrote about rumours concerning a 1978or 79 Steely Dan tour and also their alleged 1974 Warner Brothers signing.

The Floating Workshop

was a mysterious sort of record and was one of the very few that managed to make a headway into both the rock and disco worlds. Disco stations immediately picked up on the sophisticated funk of 'Black Cow', Top 40 stations picked up on the snazzy sound of 'Peg'- FM Album Oriented Rock station tuned in on 'Josie' and 'Home At Last'. Against the odds Steely Dan had triumphed and Aja succeed on as many levels that it may be the best album of the final 25 years of the 20th Century.

Rating 1 2 3 4 5 6 7 8 9 **10**

- **Peg/I Got The News (Nov. 1977)**

Finally the ice had broken for Steely Dan in the world of bubblegum pop and 'Peg' was a fine addition to the playlists of many an AM station in the winter of 1977. Led by the disco sound of Tom Scott's lyricon, Chuck Rainey's Kool & the Gang bass and Rick Marotta's out of sight funk slap drumming 'Peg' crossed over the rock/disco divide as alchemy of delight. The flipside was further confirmation of the 'Dan's acceptance of the dance floor and was sited in the lp's liner notes as a "Manhattan juke-box thump along"…exactly. Significantly both tracks featured one Mike McDonald as backing vocalist- he then riding high in his own alchemical conversion with the now Tom Johnston-less Doobie Brothers.

The Steely Dan File

Too Many Horses Heads

The "hip" rock press was very impressed with Steely Dan's continued transformation. Rolling Stone saw it as "The Second Coming of Steely Dan"[69]. High Fidelity claimed *Aja* was "easily the best album released thus far this year". Crawdaddy, once one of the leading counter-culture rags, called it simply "Steely Dan's Golden Aja". By continuing to go against the grain Fagen and Becker had become what Rolling Stone termed the "perfect anti-heroes"[70].

One of the most enlightening articles on Steely Dan in the late 1970's was Arthur

---

[69] Rolling Stone "The Second Coming od Steely Dan" by Cameron Crowe 12/28/77

[70] Rolling Stone, "Dazed at the Dude Ranch" Nov. 1977

The Floating Workshop

Lublow's "Fancy Dan" which appeared in the liberal political magazine New Times in early 1977. Lublow's article features prescient comments from various members of the 'Dan circle and seemed to illuminate the Steely Dan phenomena in the US press for the first time[71]. The article was somewhat of a highbrow piece that began with a commentary on Steely Dan music by none other than William S. Burroughs, the high priest of beat literature.

Becker and Fagen and Katz and very significantly engineer Roger Nichols had at last captured the high fidelity sound that had eluded them since *Katy Lied*[72]. Nichols' and his teams'[73] engineering efforts being re-

---

[71] Fagen , Becker and Katz had previously done in-depth interviews in the UK, namely "Art For Art's Sake" in Melody Maker in 1976

[72] In the search to restore the high fidelity sound to *Katy Lied,* the album was licensed to the new audiophile record label Mobile Fidelity and was one of their first releases in 1978. The Mobile Fidelity edition of *Katy* fetches close to $100 on the collector's market.

[73] Steely dan's engineers at the time included Al Schmitt, 1978 Grammy winner for his work on 'FM (No Static At All).

The Steely Dan File

warded in the form of a Grammy at the 1978 ceremonies in Hollywood[74].

Not ones to sit on their laurels Fagen and Becker remained active throughout 1977 and 1978 after *Aja*'s release. Through their new manager Irv Azoff Steely Dan were contracted to write and perform the theme music for an upcoming film about L.A. dj's called 'FM'. Starring Martin Mull and Cleavon Little the light hearted comedy was an abysmal failure at the box office but its' failure did little to dim the shine of Steely Dan's music in the summer of 1978. Released in May of 1978 the single from the film, 'FM (No Static At All)' maintained Steely Dan's presence in the U.S. Top 40 (it peaked at #22) and also propelled the double album soundtrack it was taken from to Platinum status for 1,000,000 copies sold.

Already in 1978 both singles culled from *Aja* , 'Peg' and 'Deacon Blues' had gone into the U.S. Top 20 and the album meanwhile had become one of the biggest sellers in the history of ABC Records, reaching as high as

---

[74] Steely Dan fans were disappointed that *Aja* didn't win the Album of the Year award, Fleetwood Mac *Rumours* took the honor that year.

The Floating Workshop

#3 on the Billboard LP chart and by the years end racking up sales in excess of 2,000,000 in the U.S. alone.

Part of *Aja*'s continues high sales in 1978 were because of a television commercial campaign launched by ABC Records. With the sultry voiced actress Eartha Kitt doing the voice over, ("Welcome to the world of Steely Dan") and an odd assortment of Fellini-esque images TV viewers were treated to an early experiment in rock video. No participation from Fagen and Becker occurred for the TV ad and if anything the Steely Dan principals continued to recede from view in the rock world as the decade came to a close.

With *Aja* making plenty of money for ABC Records, (the liner notes of the album had been written by new ABC president Steve Diener), Fagen and Becker were able to spend much of 1978 working in the field of music their real passion lied: jazz. Through a friend (Dick LaPalm), Fagen and Becker began collaboration with jazz legend Woody Herman, who was in need of material to complete an album he had begun with Chick Corea. Six Steely Dan tracks were selected by the famed big band leader to record with his new Thundering Herd big band at the Village Recorder. The album was recorded live

The Steely Dan File

during a two-day period, which Walter Becker called "the two happiest days of my life"[75].

Entitled *Chick, Donald, Walter and Woodrow*[76] the album was hugely popular in the jazz world and secured Fagen and Becker's standing as the hippest rock personalities of the decade. Several of the songs were nominated for Grammy Awards and Alan Broadbent's arrangement of 'Aja' gave the song a beautiful melodic grace.

When Woody Herman toured in 1979 and performed much of the lp's tracks it allowed people to hear Steely Dan music performed live for the first time in 5 years. For vibraphonist Victor Feldman, whose performance on Herman's dazzling version of 'Green Earrings' was perhaps the high point on the disk, it was a joyful reunion with the Thundering Herd. Feldman had left his native England in 1956 and moved to LA just to join Woody Herman's ensemble before settling in

---

[75] Rolling Stone 4/6/78 'Thundering Herd Meets Steely Dan' by Mikal Gilmore

[76] The album was recorded in the audiophile technique of Direct-to-Disk on Century Records. Many years later it was issued on CD by BBC Records.

The Floating Workshop

as LA's top jazz session player. Besides a blaring and funky rendition of 'Green Earrings' the audiophile recording also included a mysterious rendition of 'I Got The News' as well the Grammy nominated "Aja", where sax man Frank Tiberi is given a bit more space to air out than Wayne Shorter had on the original.

The production of a full-fledged jazz album was next on the Becker/Fagen agenda. The album *Apogee* marked the first official recognition of a newly signed contract Fagen and Becker had made with Warner Brothers Records and was recorded by the newly formed Pete Christlieb/Warne Marshe Quintet[77]. Produced in a neo-bebop late '40's style the album, as Fagen noted in the liner notes, was basically for "tenor freaks" and contained a nice rendition of Charlie Parker's 'Donna Lee' as well as a new Fagen and

---

[77] *Apogee* was issued at a time when Warner was issuing very few jazz albums and unfortunately was never reissued on CD. Marshe was a member of Lennie Tristano's "cool" post bop scene and this album marked his return of visibility in the jazz world. The main arranger on *Apogee* was pianist Joe Roccisano (who'd also appeared on the Woody Herman album). Roccisano would later perform a Donald Fagen track, 'Blue Lou' on the soundtrack for the film Glengarry Glenross.

The Steely Dan File

Becker track called 'Rapunzel'[78]. The critics loved it, jazz bible Downbeat gave it a rare 5 star rating and the New York Times' Robert Palmer called it "a spectacular record by anyones standards'[79]."

The year 1979 would be a year of transition for the 'Dan entourage. Tired of the lethargy of L.A. both Fagen and Becker would move back to New York. They were returning back to their home turf hoping the reality of the Big Apple would provide a new sense of musical inspiration. They had come to LA with nothing and now eight years on were recognized by many as the top rock songwriters in the country.

Part of Steely Dan's new found inspiration stemmed from the fact that they were hopeful that their original 1972 contract with ABC Records could be voided when the company was bought out by the much larger MCA Inc. in mid-1979. Citing lack of proper bookkeeping by ABC Records Fagen and

---

[78] 'Rapunzel' was based on the song 'The Land of Make Believe' by Bacharach and David

[79] *Apogee* liner notes, compiled by NY Times critic Robert Palmer

The Floating Workshop

Becker were convinced that they had been cheated by the company from the start and sought to begin work on their first album for Warner Brothers in 1979.Prior to its' demise ABC Records had released a compilation of Steely Dan singles Steely Dan/Greatest Hits 1972-1978 and as the album was a two record set Fagen and Becker deemed it as fulfilling the final obligation of their drawn out contract. The album sold extremely well hitting #30 on Billboard's LP chart, eventually attaining Platinum status (i.e.1,000,000 copies sold).

1978 Steely Dan Releases

- **Deacon Blues/Home At Last (Feb. 1978)**

A sort of unexpected hit, Deacon Blues was the longest 45 ever issued by the band, clocking it at 6:45 in its edited form. The great sax solo is by Pete Christlieb, then a member of Doc Severinson's Tonight Show band. 'Blues also featured both Larry Carlton and Lee Ritenour on guitar...some guy named Becker on bass

- **FM (No Static At All)/FM Reprise (May 1978)**

Another nod into the disco scene FM was a cool Hi-Fi sounding track featured in a terrible movie of the same name. Featuring a tasty Becker guitar solo and another big sax sound from Pete Christlieb, FM (No Static At All) was a sizable hit on urban radio and broke the Top 10 in several major markets like LA and NYC. Backing vocals are from old pal Tim Schmit, then a newly installed member of the Eagles.

- ## Josie/Black Cow (August 1978)

After their long drought of not having a hit single 1978 was almost overkill. The funky, essentially double A sided 'Josie/Black Cow' single helped Steely Dan achieve the remarkable feat of having a 45 on the US singles chart for more than 52 consecutive weeks in 1977-1978 (Cashbox charts). It also helped Steely Dan achieve a more permanent standing on the airplay charts of black and urban radio stations.

Steely Dan/Greatest Hits (December 1978)

Perhaps the best Steely Dan compilation ever- this original 2 disc set was a Platinum bestseller at the time of its release It contains all of the A-sides and many of the B-sides of all of Steely Dan's charted 45's at the time (except FM). A bonus was the charming 1976 track 'Here At The Western World'. The gatefold sleeve featured a listing of all Steely Dan personnel that had ever appeared on any 'Dan track.

Rating 1 2 3 4 5 6 7 8 **9** 10

The Floating Workshop

Expensive Kiss-off

Little was spoken of Steely Dan's contractual status as work began on album number seven in late 1979 in New York. Music was the top priority and big names were taking part in the new project. Mark Knopfler of Dire Straits was brought in to add his special touch to 'Time Out of Mind', Rick Derringer did the same on 'My Rival' and David Sanborn, Patti Austin, Hugh McCracken and of course Fagen and Becker all gave stellar performances at the now well publicized recording sessions. By the years end however the record was still only about half finished and the gremlins were taking over. Becker would be laid up after being hit by a car and contribute only sporadically throughout the final sessions[80]. Also a recording studio engineer would mistakenly erase one of the albums hottest tracks, 'The Second Arrangement'. All in all as Fagen commented

---

[80] Becker's personal life suffered greatly during this time. His girlfriend, former ABC Records staffer Karen Stanley, died of a drug overdose in January 1979 while Becker himself struggled with substance abuse problems, overcoming them as Fagen noted "by sheer Bavarian willpower."

The Steely Dan File

years later the recording of what was to become *Gaucho* was "not fun"[81]

Despite not having a record out for the second straight year Steely Dan's popularity remained high as 1980 dawned. Musician, Player and Listener magazine ran a poll among industry professionals on a wide range of categories in its' decade ending issue of December 1979 and voted Band of the Decade was none other than the Boys from Bard, Steely Dan.

All good things must come to an end it has been said and true to form the recording entity that was Steely Dan did just that in the early 1980's. As Donald Fagen put it in a 1988 interview with the Long Island newspaper Newsday[82] , "Gaucho wasn't fun, Walter was having problems, I was having life problems and the idea of what we wanted to do had become unclear".

Unclear was the appropriate word here. As worked progressed on what was to become the Gaucho album many were unclear

---

[81] Newsday 11/29/88 "After Steely Dan, Private Don" by Stephen Williams

[82] ibid

The Floating Workshop

what record company Becker and Fagen were recording the new material for. Press reports in mid-1980 wrote of Steely Dan's new album coming out on Warner Brothers, while word from MCA Records was that they'd be issuing new 'Dan product in early October.

Meanwhile the recording of the album hit a sharp snag when, as noted previously, the virtually completed track, 'The Second Arrangement, was inadvertently erased by one of the engineers. Several other songs would also be discarded for various reasons. In the end the seven completed tracks that made up the *Gaucho* album would be the final Steely Dan tracks ever completed during this first phase of Steely Dan's history. Released to radio stations by MCA on November 14, 1980, only after MCA had won a court injunction barring Steely Dan from pressing the disk on Warner Brothers[83],

Gaucho would mark the beginning of an era of higher prices for consumers. Over the objections of Becker and Fagen not to increase the list price of the album from $8.98 to $9.98 MCA went ahead and raised the

---

[83] Variety 10/28/80 "New Steely Dan Material Stays at MCA for Now"

price thus making *Gaucho* the first single LP release to bear such a price.

Several months later the band and the label were at odds once again, this time over the selection of a flipside for the single 'Time Out Of Mind'. Becker was incensed when the label put the same exact song ('Bodhisattva') on 'Mind that had been on the previous single 'Hey Nineteen', "they are crass enough to think that they can issue seven singles from this album". He later likened them to the mafia[84].

The music on *Gaucho* was as strong as ever. In fact the album contained three of Steely Dan's finest singles in 'Hey Nineteen', 'Time Out of Mind' and 'Babylon Sisters'[85], each of which became hits in 1981. Sales of the album were as strong as ever and *Gaucho* would be quickly certified Platinum for a

---

[84] Robert Klein radio interview 12/80. Becker also made a similar comment about MCA in Musician dPlayer & Listener, Jan.1981.

[85] While 'Nineteen and 'Mind would both break the US Top 40, 'Babylon Sisters' would be the bands swansong and fail to chart at all in the trade papers sales chart. Later in 1981 however 'Babylon Sisters' would hit #2 on US airplay charts.

The Floating Workshop

million copies sold, remaining in the Top 20 for much of the 1981.

By mid-1981 however it was clear that all was not well in the Steely Dan camp. Walter Becker for one was going through some very tough times; having been in a car accident outside of his Manhattan apartment in early 1980 he was now being sued by his late girlfriends mother, Lylian Wyshak.

Eventually Becker decided he needed a break from everything and moved to Hawaii, set up a recording studio and began practicing yoga. Never a social butterfly Becker now receded even further from the rock scene and was perhaps the most invisible Platinum selling artist of the early 1980's. Few people in the industry even knew what he looked like and during one episode when Becker arrived at Warner Brothers headquarters in LA to meet with the company president, the legendary Mo Ostin, the security guard refused to let him in. Becker eventually decided that he wanted to produce- and by 1984 he was working closely with China Crisis, one of the more interesting new wave bands out of the UK.

With the MCA contract now finally expired Fagen and Becker were essentially free

The Steely Dan File

to go their separate ways. Quietly at a press conference in New York on June 14, 1981 Donald Fagen announced the official end to the "group" Steely Dan.

The Steely Dan moniker appeared on some eleven Top 40 singles and eight albums that were certified Gold. Everyone from Deodato to Waylon Jennings covered their songs[86] and their unique sound would influence many groups throughout the decade ahead like Sade, Haircut 100 and Deacon Blue. But the air had grown stale at the *floating workshop,* it was time, as Fagen put it, "to do something fresh"[87].

---

[86] Jennings and Deodato both did cover versions of 'Do It Again'; the most ridiculous Steely Dan cover was undoubtably Donny & Marie's version of 'Reeling In The Years', performed live on their ABC television program circa 1978.

[87] NY Times 6/15/81,'Steely Dan Duo Going It Alone' by Robert Palmer

The Floating Workshop

1980 Steely Dan releases

- **Hey 19/Bodhissatva (live) (Nov.1980)**

A strong selling hit single 'Hey 19' was Steely Dan's 5th consecutive US Top 40 hit and helped propel the parent album to the top of the LP charts in late 1980. A cool, funky sort of number with Lolita-esque lyrics, '19 received airplay on urban and album rock stations and demonstrated the 'Dan's crossover appeal yet again. The flipside was a flashback to the hippie days of 1974 and featured a long drunken intro by one Jerome Aniton- who apparently believed Fagen's real name was Mr. Stevie Dan! Whatever.

Gaucho (November 1980)

Although mostly New York recorded Gaucho represented Steely Dan's ode to Hollywood and it's mythology. A slick and perfect set it lacked the dreaminess of Aja. The rhythms and the arrangements hold this set together and much credit must go to the production and engineering team led by Katz & Nichols. Guest stars included Mark Knopfler, Rick Derringer, David Sanborn and Valerie Simpson. Cool.

Rating 1 2 3 4 5 6 7 **8** 9 10

True Companions

True Companions

1981-1999

The Steely Dan File

True Companions

With the official demise of Steely Dan in 1981 the careers of Walter Becker and Donald Fagen continued, however sporadically on into the 1990's. While Fagen moved on with a successful solo career, Becker moved on to the production and engineering side and by the end of the 1980's both had secured themselves distinct niches in the music biz. These niches in turn would enable the dynamic duo to return once again as Steely Dan at the dawn of the Clinton Era in the early 1990's.

Fagen's solo career began almost immediately upon the demise of Steely Dan with 1982's *The Nightfly*, which by all accounts was a brilliant album and is to many the definitive recording of the cd age. Like *Aja*, the *Nightfly* had the right musicians in just the right place- like a fine bossa nova album it triumphed in understatement and melody. Produced by Katz and recorded and

The Steely Dan File

mixed by Roger Nichols using digital equipment *The Nightfly* shined like few others would in the 1980's. The eight song epic included performances from many of the previous 'Dan alumni: Porcaro, Gadd, Carlton, McCracken and lyrically according to Fagen represented "certain fantasies that might have been entertained by a young man growing up in the remote suburbs of a northeastern city during the late '50's and early '60's".[88]

---

[88] Liner notes of *The Nightfly*

True Companions

Though nominated for seven Grammy Awards *The Nightfly* failed to win even one at the 1983 ceremonies. Fagen could perhaps take heart knowing that he had helped launch the career of the big winner that night, Jeff Porcaro and his band Toto. Although Porcaro himself seemed bewildered when he copped the Best Producer award and stated that the award "belongs to Gary Katz".[89]

Two hit singles emerged from *The Nightfly* both of which conjured up nostalgic optimism from the era of John F. Kennedy's presidency. The album's lead single (which peaked at #17 on the US charts[90]) was the oddly titled 'IGY (What A Beautiful World)' a song that chronicled the International Geophysical Year, a period when scientists around the world tested, studied and predicted how science and technology would be used and benefit mankind (June 1957-

---

[89] Grammy Awards broadcasts Feb.1983. Porcaro would die tragically in 1992 from resperatory problems caused from a combination of pesticides (he was working in his garden at the time of his death) and cocaine abuse.

[90] Cashbox Top 40. 'IGY' stalled at #26 for four weeks on Billboards chart.

The Steely Dan File

July1958). The song's optimism was a departure for the Steely Dan sound and conjured up a sense of halcyon days-like mentality now long forgotten.

The follow-up single, 'The New Frontier', told the tale of a Brubeck fan and a Tuesday Weld look-alike squirreled away in a fall out shelter that had been built "in case the Reds decide to push the button down". To promote 'The New Frontier' Warner Brothers had a video made which nicely brought to the screen the imagery of 1962 suburbia, but alas failed to feature the reclusive Fagen. The video was eventually released, in a limited edition, as a cd video in the late 1980's, having been a minor hit on the popular cable TV network MTV.

Reclusive or not Fagen's lack of visibility didn't stop his first solo disc from selling well. *The Nightfly* would climb to #11 on the Billboard album chart and become a Gold disc for 500,000 copies sold in mid-1983. Great sales figures when one considers that Fagen's only line of promotion was a series of press interviews and a one-off concert at a small nightclub on Long Island.

The Nightfly's successful chart run came against the backdrop of the so-called second

True Companions

"British Invasion". New wave British acts like Culture Club, Haircut 100 and the Human League had splashed upon the US shores with slick hit singles and a youthful exuberance. Many of these UK acts would site Steely Dan as an influence over the course of the 1980's, one Deacon Blue, even copping their name from a classic 'Dan track. Perhaps one of the oddest cover versions came from Howard Jones who enlisted none other than 'Reeling In the Years' guitarist Elliot Randall when he did his own version of 'IGY' in 1992. Others who specifically stated their love of the 'Dan included Joe Jackson, Nick Heyward and soon to be supergroup Tears For Fears.

So as the Reagan years plodded on it was apparent that Steely Dan's music was still relevant and vibrant to many of the young pop bands and listeners now buying compact discs instead of vinyl. A crossover appeal still existed as evidence in the 1983 remake of Steely Dan's first hit single, 'Do It Again'. An oddly mixed medley of 'Do It Again" and Michael Jackson's "Billie Jean" stormed up the European and UK charts during the summer of '83'. A pair of Italian dj's who went by the name of Clubhouse even placed the song in the BBC Top 10..some 30 notches higher than Steely Dan's own version ever made when it was issued in Britain as a single in 1972 and 1975.

With the industry switch to compact discs Steely Dan continued to make money for both Fagen and Becker as well as MCA Records. MCA capitalized on the Steely Dan sound by having Roger Nichols remaster the entire Steely Dan library for digital sound in 1982. One of the first releases was a very good compilation named simply *Decade* (MCA 1985), a cd that would go platinum within a year of its release.

After a four year hiatus Walter Becker returned to the music seen in early 1985 as producer and keyboardist for the Liverpool based China Crisis, another new wave act greatly influenced, at least inspirationally by the 'Dan of Steel. Led by guitarist Eddie Lundon and vocalist Garry Daly China Crisis were an exciting young band that had first came to prominence in 1982 with the new wave hit 'African and White'.

China Crisis' 1983 Steely influenced "Working with Fire and Steel" had been picked up by Warner Brothers in the US and through the label came to the attention of Becker. Soon after, Becker contacted the group to see if they'd be interested in working with him. The band was overjoyed, a deal was struck, and Becker flew to England to oversee

True Companions

the sessions for the *Flaunt The Imperfection* album. The result was one of the best new wave music albums of the '80's and in England at least, a commercial success, spawning three Top 20 hits and hitting #9 on the UK album charts.

A year later in 1986 a Steely Dan reunion of sorts took place when Gary Katz got Fagen and Becker to both appear on model-turned singer Rosie Vela's debut release *Zazu*, which Katz was producing in LA. Longtime Steely pal Rick Derringer also played on the record which, despite strong support, got little radio airplay and sold few copies for A&M Records.

New solo material from Donald Fagen meanwhile was put on hold in 1987 as he decided against releasing newly recorded material that Warner Brothers (and his devout following) were hoping would be his second solo album. Instead Fagen delved into a soundtrack project for the film 'Bright Lights, Big City'. From that album came the minor, yet, popular, hit 'Century's End' in 1988.

As the 1980's closed Walter Becker continued to hone his production skills, now working closely with engineer extraordinaire Roger (The Immortal) Nichols. Two slick pro-

The Steely Dan File

ductions emerged in 1989 from the pair. The first was Becker's second collaboration with China Crisis, the sparkling *Diary of A Hollow Horse*, which featured several Becker guitar solos.

The second Becker/Nichols effort was an interesting neo-folk set from Rickie Lee Jones entitled *Flying Cowboys*, which put Jones in the US Top 40 for the first time in several years. The China Crisis album on the other had was a bust, even in England, and led to the bands break-up, though they did return in the mid-'90's with an inspired Steely Dan sounding *Warped By Success*.

True Companions

1980's Donald Fagen & Steely Dan Releases

- ## True Companion (Nov.1981)

A fine debut track from Fagen- atmospheric, futuristic, oddly issued as a 45 with former Eagle Don Felder on the flipside, Smooth,prelude to Kamakiriad..a gift for us here in the 21st Century.

Gold (June 1982)

Not popular when issued in 1982, Gold is still nevertheless a fine album. How can you argue with a set that gives you FM, Green Earrings and Babylon Sisters?

1 2 3 4 5 6 7 **8** 9 10

The Steely Dan File

- **IGY (what A beautiful World)/Walk Between The Raindrops (Nov. 1982)**

A pleasant addition to the US Top 40 in the fall of '82, 'IGY' grooved along with snappy nostalgic charm. The flipside grooved along-sounding like a cover version of some obscure 1962 song.

The Nightfly (November 1982)

Fagen jumped into his solo career with this perfect collage of New Frontier America. Fagen awakened a memory long forgotten by the baby-boomers and brought us to the origin of the Steely Dan philosophy. Jazz, bossa nova, JFK, radio, women all made up the youthful Fagen…a concept album….that worked on almost every level.

Rating 1 2 3 4 5 6 7 8 **9.5** 10

- **The New Frontier/Ruby Baby (Jan. 1983)**

A groovy follow-up single to 'IGY', 'The New Frontier' was Fagen's lone attempt to puncture the MTV scene. Although not a chart success, 'Frontier showed that Fagen could spin a more or less straightforward yarn in a pop song. The flipside, 'Ruby Baby' was a truly brilliant cover of the old Drifters classic.

True Companions

Decade (August 1985)

To many this is the best greatest hits collection, re-mastered, a ton of tracks-including the LP version of FM, East St.Louis, Josie, My Old School….pity about the cover though.

1 2 3 4 5 6 7 8 **9** 10

- **Century's End/Shanghai Confidential (Feb.1988)**

A catchy track from the soundtrack of the film Bright Lights, Big City, Nice enough, but we wanted more…

The Steely Dan File

A Rock n Soul Reunion

While Becker continued to work behind the scenes as a producer Fagen took an unexpected turn toward the public spotlight as the 1980's closed. It would be a sign of things to come. For the first time since 1974 Fagen began performing in a series of live concerts in the autumn of 1989. Under the banner 'The New York Rock 'n Soul Revue' Fagen, along with the likes of Patti Austin, Phoebe Snow and Mike McDonald, led the 'Revue in a "greatest hits" type concert series complete with spontaneous jams and wry one-liners. Fans were overjoyed and crowded the small New York nightclubs where the entourage performed.

The popularity of the shows led to the release of the crisply recorded *Live At The*

True Companions

Beacon in 1991 and (with the addition of Becker on guitar) a sold out summer tour in 1992. Finally fans were able to hear some Steely Dan songs in a concert setting. Fagen and Becker were taking note and were happily shocked at fan reaction.

By the end of '92 with Becker now working even more closely with Fagen (as his producer) it was clear that the days of Steely Dan were far from "gone forever" or "over a long time ago" as their song 'Pretzel Logic' stated. On the contrary, the new era of Steely Dan III was beginning, an era that would show that the titanic Steely Dan were returning from the dead and were alive, and very well thank you, in America.

The return of Steely Dan came about in a very organic and unpretentious manner. As Fagen continued with his small concerts at New York City nightclubs he began to become aware of just how starved people were to hear Steely Dan songs in concert. With the encouragement of his future wife Libby Titus and booking agent Pete Fogel Fagen began to open his mind to playing songs that he himself had long ago stopped listening to.

Becker's reunion with Fagen came about quite by accident and almost totally due to audience support. At a packed Friday night Rock n Soul Revue concert at the midtown Lonestar Roadhouse it was discovered that Becker was in the audience. Soon he was almost carried by the audience up to the stage- a guitar was tossed into his hands- an impromptu version of the 1978 hit 'Josie' soon followed. From that spontaneous reunion a new day had dawned in the world of Steely Dan. Soon Fagen officially enlisted Becker to produce his new album, the tentatively, *Tea House On the Tracks* at River Sound studios in New York. As the year 1993 dawned it was evident that the world of Steely Dan was far from being eclipsed into a world of inconsequential rock footnotes. In fact the careers of both Donald Fagen and Walter Becker were now on a plateau of rewarding artistic aspirations.

January 1993 saw Mr. Fagen performing live again at his favorite New York club, the Lonestar in midtown. Fagen's appearance there came under the bill 'Libby Titus' New York Nights' and saw him collaborate with guitarist Pat Metheny, among others. (The shows organizer incidentally, the aforementioned Ms. Titus, would soon become Mrs. Donald Fagen at a ceremony in Manhattan). No new songs were played at the January

True Companions

gigs but press reports soon after hinted that Fagen's long awaited (11 years!) follow up to The Nightfly was nearing completion.

In May of '93 it must have seemed like Christmas to long neglected Steely Dan fans as news of the imminent release of Fagen's new album was joined with the announcement that Steely Dan, the "group", would be undertaking a major US tour during the summer. Collaboration with Walter Becker had apparently gone so well during the recording of Fagen's new album that it was decided that a series of concerts, as Steely Dan, would be worthwhile.

The revitalized Becker, now a yoga practitioner and Hawaiian resident, had become such a prominent force on Fagen's disc as producer, guitarist and bass player that he was able to secure a deal to cut his own solo album for Giant Records, a record label headed by Steely Dan's one time manager Irv Azoff. Along with session man Drew Zing, Becker would handle guitar chores on the Steely Dan tour. Becker would also debut some solo material that for the first time would feature himself on lead vocals.

Donald Fagen's album meanwhile finally hit the record shops on Tuesday May 25th,

The Steely Dan File

1993. Carrying the curious title *Kamakiriad,* the eight-track set was trumpeted by the music press (Billboard 4/2/93) as an epic of Steely Dan proportions. Lyrically centering on the travels of a turn of the millennium driver whose life "began yesterday when they brought my kamakiri" Kamakiriad presented the listener with the perfect bookend to *The Nightfly*. Whereas *The Nightfly* concerned the coming of age an individual in the late 1950's *Kamakiriad* jumped ahead some forty years, detailing the experiences of a still somewhat uncertain persona, now goggled and cruising the hazardous 'Trans-island Skyway' in his kamakiri to his ultimate stop at 'The Teahouse on the tracks'.

Much of the recording of *Kamakiriad* took place at River Sound Studios in New York, the studio Fagen co-owned with Gary Katz. Additional recording took place at Becker's Hyperbolic Sound studios in Hawaii and the engineering, done to perfection once more, was overseen by Roger Nichols.

The Steely Dan tour of 1993 began in mid-August and was without question a success. The San Francisco Chronicle saw it as "the summer's most anticipated concert event" and tickets for the Madison Square

True Companions

Garden show sold out in 40 minutes. Sold out gigs from Jones Beach on Long Island to Mountain View in Northern California were punctuated by the wit, candor and music professionalism that was uniquely Steely Dan. As the New York Times Jon Pareles put it, "It may be a reunion tour, but with Steely Dan the payoff is in craftmanship not nostalgia."

The return of Steely Dan was not without its critics however, Rolling Stone gave the tour very little coverage and rated Fagen's new album as an only so-so project. In fact the album was virtually ignored by the radio world causing the lead single 'Tomorrow's Girls' to fail to chart at all on Billboard's Hot 100. While *Kamakiriad* did become a Gold disc it sold only sporadically and fell off the album chart quickly after the Steely Dan tour finished up in late September in Albany, New York.

As 1993 closed MCA Records had finally compiled a long awaited definitive Steely Dan compilation "boxed set" in *Citizen Dan*, a four cd set that included everything the group had officially put out (sans 'Dallas' and 'Sail The Waterway'), plus a demo of 'Everyone's Gone to The Movies'. MCA was happy to have

The Steely Dan File

Steely Dan on their roster; all of Steely Dan's album had continued to sell throughout the '80's and '90s and all of the original albums (except Countdown To Ecstasy) were now certified Platinum (i.e. at least 1 million copies sold).

Asia beckoned Steely Dan as the spring of 1994 dawned. Long the subject of Steely imagery and lyrics the orient hosted the 1994 version of the Steely Dan Orchestra with a series of sold out shows in Japan in April. Soon after, US cities missed in '93 were toured by the 'Dan ensemble and in September Walter Becker's much anticipated solo debut was issued.

Eleven Tracks of Whack was Becker laid bare. Minimally produced (by Steely Dan standards) at Becker's Hawaiian outpost *Whack* delved into dark episodes of drug addiction, depression and living on the edge, all episodes Becker had himself experienced over the course of his 20 year musical career. It took critics and fans alike by surprise and as a result fell into a commercial oblivion. Musically the album was a gem of funk, mantra and pop and even had a touch of family life ('Little Kawaii') that no Steely Dan album could ever possess.

True Companions

Not dismayed in the least by the commercial failure of 'Whack Fagen and Becker drove on in 1995 to compile the first ever official live Steely Dan album. Culled from best performances of the 1993 and 1994 shows *Alive In America* dazzled in sound with great licks from Drew Zing (on a jazzed up version of 'Peg'), Dennis Chambers (with a funked up drum solo on 'Josie') and Becker (on a sterling version of the 1973 classic 'Bodhisattva').

Promoting the album upon its' release in late 1995 Steely Dan made their first live TV appearance ever with a spot on David Letterman's Late Night and also hosted a live radio program from New York City and performed 'Dan tracks never before performed live like 'East St.Louis Toodle oo' and 'Bad Sneakers'. Sales for *Alive In America*, which was issued on Giant Records, were good and it placed Steely Dan back in the US album charts for the first time in over a decade.

A devout Steely Dan following was emerging on the Internet and in publications like 'Metal Leg', a popular fan 'zine. Metal Leg had been founded in England by researcher Brian Sweet and had been taken over by New York photographer Pete Fogel. Sweet would publish the first book on Steely Dan in 1994, 'Reeling' In The Years' (Omnibus Press) while Fogel would actually go on tour with the band as photographer and chronicler.

Steely Dan themselves would counter their fans adoration with a series of tongue in cheek web sites that would prove once and for all that they were the funniest band around. In 1994 they did an online interview with fans and Becker himself would periodically answer fans' e-mails at the steelydan.com website.

Fagen and Becker had timidly begun recording again as Steely Dan in early 1996 but they seemed uncertain as to whether it would lead to anything. Instead they decided to dust off a few of their own personal favorite 'Dan songs and re-work them. The resulting Art Crimes tour in the summer of 1996 was a critical success and featured gratifying new versions of 'Do It Again', 'Midnite Cruiser', 'Rikki' and 'Everyone's Gone To the Movies'. Although a few new songs were performed during the tour, it was obvious that new Steely Dan music was not a priority. Not yet.

The Fagen and Becker team, unlike many rock partnerships, was still ticking

True Companions

three decades on.. As the century drew to a close folks in the Steely Dan camp were abuzz with news about the first new Steely Dan album in twenty years. In late December of 1999, a week before the century's end radio stations in the US were given promo copies of several new Steely Dan tracks. From the initial listen to the new songs it was obvious to all that Steely Dan were back. Like a slip in time they had managed to cross the diamond with the pearl once more.

The Steely Dan File

1990's Steely Dan Releases

Live At The Beacon (October 1991)

A bright fun collection of pop songs- pulled together by Fagen and his future wife Libby Titus. Now free from his 'Dan persona Fagen conducted his show with an appearance that looked straight out of Blackboard Jungle. IGY indeed.

Rating 1 2 3 4 5 6 7 **8** 9 10

Kamakiriad (May 1993)

A US Top 10 hit, Kamakiriad is a groove-infected spectacle that combined mid-life doubts with Bard flashbacks. Becker's bass never sounded better and his guitar is also in top form. Fagen's keyboards were getting funkier and the Weather Report style jam at the end of 'Dunes captures nicely the early '90's 'Dan sound. This set includes one Fagen/Becker track, as well as one Fagen/Titus song.

Rating 1 2 3 4 5 6 7 **8** 9 10

True Companions

Eleven Tracks of Whack (September 1994)

This moody set of rhythms and drum machines didn't go over well with many in the 'Dan audience. What makes it stand up though is Becker's latent sense of funk and his above average lyricism. High point: the wonderfully brooding 'This Moody Bastard'. It seems to be the one disc that really is able to stand apart from the whole 'Dan sound...like fine wine...it gets better with age.

Rating 1 2 3 4 5 6 **7.5** 8 9 10

Alive In America (October 1995)

Sort of a live greatest hits, Alive In America, documents the Steely Dan band sound of the early 90's. Highlights include a jazzed up 'Peg' a funky 'Josie' and a surreal 'IGY'-esque version of 'Reeling In The Years'.

Rating 1 2 3 4 5 6 **7** 8 9 10

Back to 'Nature

Back To 'Nature

2000-present

The Steely Dan File

Back to 'Nature

Astrologers call the 28 year cycle from birth to maturity, a 'Saturn Return". It means basically that the planet Saturn, harbinger of doom and gloom, but also an agent of profound change and understanding, is returning to the exact spot that it inhabited at one's birth.

The year 2000 marked such an event in the life of Steely Dan. Twenty-eight years after dazzling the pop charts with *Can't Buy A Thrill* and 'Do It Again', Fagen and Becker were trying to re-connect with an audience that it had only marginally ac-

The Steely Dan File

knowledged during it's eventful lifetime. Likewise the media world, once deprived of the quirky New York pop stars was about to embrace the 'Dan of Steel' with warm platitudes long overdue.

A Stellar "Saturn Return"

For starters Steely Dan's Saturn return would mark the first time since the Nixon Administration that Steely Dan would be mounting a tour to coincide with the release of their new studio album. This would be the first time since 1974 that a Steely Dan album of new material would be complimented with a live interpretation.

Amid much anticipation the new Steely Dan orchestra was unveiled at a New York City concert in late January of 2000. And in a sure sign that this was a Saturn Return of great significance the concert was being filmed for a PBS documentary, Steely Dan were *real* musicians....a far cry from their first TV appearance 28 years earlier, lip-synching to 'Do It Again' on Dick Clark's American Bandstand.

Finally on the last day of February 2000, *Two Against Nature* was issued by Giant Records, the cool music company run by by Steely Dan's one-time manager Irv Azoff[91]. It was a release unlike

---

[91] Although affiliated with Warner Brothers Records in the US, Giant Records in other parts of the world was distributed by BMG Records.

Back to 'Nature

any other in Steely Dan history, as it was supported by the large, advertising conglomeration (the internet, cable TV, satellite radio etc) that simply didn't exist in the Carter Administration. Devoted Steely Dan fans were unnerved a bit when literally overnight *Two Against Nature* went from a hotly discussed item on Steely Dan web pages to a *Today* show and USA Today topic of discussion.

After a few false starts the Steely Dan machine had completed their first new, fully authentic, bonafide *Steely Dan* album in 20 years in mid 1999. The album was a 9-track set and was led by the single 'Cousin Dupree', which was released to radio stations in December of 1999. Three other tracks were eventually also issued as cd singles, 'Jack of Speed', 'What A Shame About Me' and 'Janie Runaway'.

It had been a long time since 'Hey Nineteen' had lumbered up the Top 40 chart and while 'Cousin Dupree' did break the Adult Contemporary airplay list, it didn't even chart on the Billboard Hot 100 "singles" chart". But it was a bouncy, upbeat blues number with definitive 'Dan noire lyrics that Fagen described as a "rural narrative"[92]. Thanks to the Internet the song could be heard by fans worldwide before the New Year, with fans posting mp3 recordings of it on various websites.

---

[92] VH-1 Storytellers interview

The Steely Dan File

The release of the parent album against a backdrop of unprecedented publicity gave *Two Against Nature* a high debut of #6 in its' first week of release, by far Steely Dan's highest debut position ever. The album was *hot*, not only because it was good, or that it was by Steely Dan, but also that it was their first new album in twenty years. Steely Dan were now public domain -everybody from E! Entertainment to VH-1 wanted a piece of them.

Fagen and Becker handled this new era of Steely Dan scrutiny with the quiet sense of class that always put them apart from their contemporaries. In fact the success of *Two Against Nature* was the result of their deliberate step-by-step process of rehabilitation that had began ten years ago during the *Kamakiriad* sessions. A reunion was followed by a sound thrashing out of the Steely Dan songbook during the tours of '93, '94 and '96, a re-grouping and finally a great plunge into being Steely Dan in the studio...again.

It was no surprise that their contemporaries, namely The Eagles and the Doobie Brothers, were not having the same success or re-invention. By 2000 the Eagles were struggling to creep out from underneath their highly publicized 1994 reunion aura and record even a handful of new songs. It was not easy trying to sound relevant when your past was always right there staring you in the face. The Doobies meanwhile had trouble maintaining relevance after an early '90's hit, 'The Doctor', put

Back to 'Nature

them back in the Top 10. Now led once again by Tom Johnston, the Doobie Brothers of the 1990's had neither the Skunk nor McDonald and by the end of the decade were playing Reno rather than Madison Square Garden.

The publicity for *Two Against Nature*, which startled many a slumbering 'Dan fan, came fast and furious. Even before the album had been issued Steely Dan were appearing in a televised concert at the Manhattan Sony Sound Studios in midtown. The concert was soon after broadcast nationwide by the PBS television network. For a group that had made only 1 national television since 1973 this was an earth-shattering event.

For Steely Dan, the return seemed natural and the puppet masters Fagen and Becker made the most of their new found acclaim. After the PBS concert there was more to follow: a q & a mini-concert on Vh-1, in which audience members could pepper Becker & Fagen with questions about their songs etc. A live appearance on the top rated night program Late Night with David Letterman on the CBS network took place in March of 2000.

A month later on NBC viewers woke up one Friday morning to see Fagen and Becker et al, up early for a chilly morning concert in Rockefeller Plaza. *Today* show host Katy Couric seemed really perplexed by Fagen and Becker as they delved into classic tracks 'Peg', 'Green Earrings'

The Steely Dan File

and 'Black Friday', songs which only a few years before could be heard only on cd or vinyl. Sure, Katy Couric, was oblivious to the fact that Fagen had released two Gold albums and Becker had been producing for sixteen years during their twenty year "hiatus", it was pretty cool to wake up to 'Black Friday', 'Kid Charlemagne' and 'Cousin Dupree".

Needless to say the publicity helped and *Two Against Nature*, led by the radio single, 'Cousin Dupree', soon was certified as a Platinum album, Steely Dan's first since the *Decade* compilation of 1985.. '*Nature* would remain a consistent seller for two years and spawn a handful of airplay hits including 'Janie Runaway' and 'Jack of Speed', one of the songs that Steely Dan had debuted back in the 1996 Art Crimes Tour.

The aforementioned PBS concert would eventually also be released on video and DVD and see Steely Dan put in their first showing on the video chart. *Two Against Nature* was eventually issued under various incarnations (including DVD Audio) and even showed up on vinyl in the European market.

The Steely Dan tour meanwhile went from strength to strength with sold out shows in New York, LA, San Francisco and eventually even London, Dublin and Stockholm. The band, rooted by the excellent rhythm section of Tom Barney on bass, Ted Baker on piano and Keith Carlock on

Back to 'Nature

drums, was now complimented nicely by the dazzling new guitarist John Herington. Herington had an almost Larry Carlton type edge to his solos and he matched up nicely with the "reluctant guitar god"[93] Becker. Fagen meanwhile had now morphed nicely into a Ray Charles-esque mc, while the horn section was under the helm of the great Cornelius Bumpus and at times the spectacular Chris Potter. A trio of beautiful female background singers rounded out the pop fusion ensemble nicely. This is not to say the critics were silent or that in some of the outer lying suburbs (where jazz was probable non-existent) Steely Dan had trouble filling the seats. Bruce Westbrook of the Houston Chronicle found *Two Against Nature* lacked Steely Dan's "former zeal and exploration"[94] and that it suffered from, "mellow monotony, compounded by the undistinctiveness of it's songs".

Criticism like this was irrelevant to Steely Dan at this point and three episodes would take place in the wake of *'Two Against Nature's* success that sealed their fame as true pioneers of pop and rock music. And in true Saturn Return nature these episodes forced Steely Dan to face the most important

---

[93] 'Return of the dark Soul Brothers Rolling Stone Feb, 2000

[94] Houston Chronicle, March 12, 2000 p.6 'Steely Dan Lost In Groove'

obstacle that had kept them from being the best the could be: public acclaim and visibility.

2000 Steely Dan Releases

Two Against Nature (February 2000)

Steely Dan's triumphant return, Two Against Nature, seamlessly added it self to the 'Dan library almost as if there had been a slip in time. Two decades after Gaucho Steely Dan was back as if nothing had changed: bass, drums, keyboards...tight....horns: impeccable...guitars: snazzy, vocals/lyrics: amazingly worthy...short stories meet semi-autobiography...Burroughs would be proud.

1 2 3 4 5 6 7 **8** 9 10

Two Against Nature (DVD) (December 2000)

Filmed originally as a PBS concert documentary, this DVD shows the band in fine form as they warmed up for their 2000 US/UK tour. It's worth watching just to hear the boys witty banter in between the songs- hilarious give and take with 'Dan guru Pete Fogel...funny stuff with sax man Bumpus. Fagen looks like a cross between Allen Ginsburg and Ray Charles!

Back to 'Nature

And The Award Goes To...

Over the years Steely Dan's relationship with the Grammy world had been somewhat baffling. After debuting with two stunning hit singles in 1972, they were passed over as *Best New Artist* nominees by the likes of Maureen McGovern, Marie Osmond and Bette Midler (the eventual winner). A year later they received their first song nomination when 'Rikki Don't Lose That Number' was nominated as *Best Pop Vocal Performance* only to lose to Paul McCartney and his 'Band on the Run'.

Three years later in 1977 the epic *Aja* received 3 Grammy nominations, including *Album of the Year* and *Best Pop Vocal Performance* but had to settle for the technical award of *Best Engineered (non-Classical)*. Likewise in 1978 and 1980 they had to take

The Steely Dan File

solace with the same award, for "*FM*" and *Gaucho*.

Finally in 1982 it seemed the tide would turn when Donald Fagen's brilliant *The Nightfly* was nominated for 7 Grammy Awards, including the prestigious *Album of the Year* award. Yet in one of those twists of quirky fate the Grammy's were dominated that year by the pop drivel of Toto, founded by one-time 'Dan drummer Jeff Porcaro. *Album of the Year, Record of the Year* even *Producer of the Year* all went to the band named after the dog in Wizard of Oz. A decade later it was perhaps a little less insulting when Fagen's *Kamakiriad* lost the *Album of the Year*, it's only nomination, to Whitney Houston's *Bodyguard* soundtrack.

So when the National Academy of Recording Arts and Sciences announced four nominations for *Two Against Nature* few in the Steely Dan world raised an eyebrow. Shockingly, even to themselves Steely Dan walked away with all four awards, including the coveted album of the year award.

In what marked their first ever-live television appearance Fagen and Becker, along with engineer Roger Nichols marched up to the stage and happily snatched their Grammy Awards, which many believed would go to controversial rapper, Eminem. On pick-

Back to 'Nature

ing up their first of four Grammy Awards, Fagen quipped, "We've been around a while, it's nice to get one of these."

In wake of their Grammy success Steely Dan's accolades continued with a ceremony at the Rock n Roll Hall of Fame in Cleveland, Ohio. With Moby acting as presenter, Becker and Fagen stumbled up to the stage and spouted off some witty banter about the Mothers Of Invention before accepting their Hall of Fame induction. Needless to say it seemed odd to see Steely Dan in the presence of Bono, Robbie Robertson and other rock personas and it was even more interesting to see the likes of Queen's Brian May jamming with them on 'Do It Again', with Paul Schaeffer on keyboards of no less.

Steely Dan had morphed into a marketable commodity. Press interviews were many, if predictable. The Guardian's Barney Hoskins called them "librarians of acid[95] "and delved into Steely Dan's ironic and Philip K. Dick type mindset. But Middle America got the usual blathering about Steely Dan's 1970's history and how it took TWO Decades for them to complete their follow-up

---

[95] 'Countdown To Ecstasy", The Guardian, Feb. 28, 2000

The Steely Dan File

to the Reagan era *Gaucho* (released Nov.14, 1980).

Perhaps the one accolade that Steely Dan got in 2001 that really made an impression on them came from the Berklee School of Music in Boston. The legendary school, long supporters on the study of the music of Steely Dan (they had begun offering courses that cover Fagen & Becker's songs as early as 1979), was once Fagen's alma mater and has a reputation on par with MIT among music students. In receiving Honorary Doctorates from the school Becker and Fagen were finally speechless and quite pleased that they had made a mark in arena that they could make a significant impact: education.

As 2001 closed Steely Dan had actually climbed to the top of the rock world for the first time. A multi-platinum album and hugely successful world tour had now been crowned by Honorary Doctorates, induction into the Hall of Fame and the unexpected victory of four Grammy Awards All of this public acclaim led Fagen to quip that they would soon be returning to their lives as "shut-ins".[96]

---

[96] CBS-TV Grammy Awards telecast Feb. 2001

Back to 'Nature

Time To 'Go

It would be into New York City recording studios that Fagen and Becker would be shut in to during the latter half of 2001. A bunch of new songs were pounded out at the Record Plant In Manhattan. Guest pianist, noted Blue Note artist, Bill Charlap made for a groove-inflected compliment to Fagen's soulful Hammond organ sound. Becker's guitar, vocal and lyrics made for some distinctive Kerouac-ian beat pop, while the tight drumming of Keith Carlock and the powerful groove driven bass of Tom Barney, along with the finesse guitar work of John Herington made for a full aural masterpiece, similar to 1976's *Royal Scam*.

Titled '*Everything Must Go*' when it was issued in June of 2003 (now on Reprise), Steely Dan 9th studio album marked an end in no uncertain terms. Particularly poignant was the title track, which amalgamated an old Fagen rhythm[97] on top of a Coltrane-

---

[97] 'Everything Must Go' borrowed heavily from Fagen's 1988 song 'Big Noise, New York', which was never issued on any Fagen album, but appeared on a European cd single.

The Steely Dan File

esque orchestration. The lyrics were commentary from the native New York voice of the Steely Dan persona on the end of an era, an end embodied in the tragedy of September 11, 2001.

While other tracks were not as melancholy as the title track, they were in a sense a celebration of the people who don't exactly have everything going their way, the losers in life. By countering these Bukoski-ian themes with a full Blue Note sound system Fagen and Becker had created perhaps the perfect bookend to their 1972 volume of dark halcyon dreams 'Can't Buy A Thrill.

While reviews for *Everything Must Go* were generally strong when it was issued in the spring of 2003- it's release seemed to catch the cd buying public off guard. After debuting at #6 in Billboard, EMG slid quickly down the chart, marking Steely Dan's poorest showing for a studio album in thirty years. No doubt the lack of a Steely Dan friendly radio format didn't help matters- Steely Dan was too witty for "smooth jazz", to jazzy for "adult contemporary" and too old to be "alternative".

The poor cd sales aside Steely Dan in 2003 had a very successful year when they undertook another US tour.

Back to 'Nature

Adding some of their obscure older back catalogue, ("Monkey In Your Soul", "Sign In Stranger") and letting Becker take some lead vocals made for a very enjoyable night out for US concertgoers.

Soon after the close of the *Everything Must Go* tour tragedy struck when Steely Dan's saxophonist, Cornelius Bumpus, died of a heart attack at his home in California. Soon after Donald Fagen suffered the terrible loss of his mother Eleanor.

Fagen Morphs-Becker Takes another Whack

After their successful 2003 tour and in wake of their unexpected success with Two Against Nature it would have been perfectly acceptable for Steely Dan to close it's chapter in the annals of rock. They were award winning songwriters, platinum selling rock stars and now after a decade as a touring ensemble they were recognized as fascinating and funny live attraction. What more could Fagen and Becker have to say? What more could they want to stay?

For Fagen their were several things that he needed to exorcise from his self- and fortunately for music lovers he was able to manifest these feelings in a snazzy solo al-

The Steely Dan File

bum, recorded over the two year period of 2004 and 2005.

On a personal front Fagen had suffered through the tragic Alzheimer's demise of his mother Eleanor Fagen (nee' Rosenberg) in 2004. Her death brought to front many thoughts on "the man in the brite nitegown" and led to Fagen conceiving his new solo disc as the third part in his solo saga. *The Nightfly* encapsuled the hopes and dreams of a youngster, *Kamakiriad* reflected the panic of middle age and the uniquely titled 2006 release *Morph the Cat*, brought out the hopes and fears of Fagen's later years.

A Political Cat

In so many ways Fagen's solo effort materialized as a reaction to having been silent for so many years politically and culturally. Sure Steely Dan was almost always seen as a embodying some sort of liberal ideal, but they never were specific.

Having lived through the horrors of September 11, 2001 and the subsequent reaction by US politicians and the public in general Fagen had a great need to exorcise some demons- he was a Manhattanite after

Back to 'Nature

all; 911 was a local tragedy- one that struck home- literally.

Morph the Cat was a dazzling return for Fagen- an album full of groove inflected sarcastic ramblings about what it is like to live in post 9-11 NYC. Reflecting on age, politics, death and intellect Fagen now stood head and shoulders above his contemporaries and the younger generations of pop music drivel. After years of hiding his opinions and personal life Fagen had managed to shed his shy persona and get a few digs in at the Bush Administration et al.

Featuring a rhythm section of Freddie Washington (bass) and Keith Carlock (drums) and Fagen (Fender piano) *Morph the Cat* was a funky collage that reflects the feelings of Manhattanhite Fagen as he approached life's autumnal years. But *Morph* was no whining Woody Allen monologue, instead Fagen had pulled in the listener with an enjoying sense that life can still be made fun of and cast in sarcastic light regardless of whether the world around us is smoldering in the ignorance of early 21st century America.

Apocalypse Wow

After 2003's *Everything Must Go* many had written off Fagen and the Steely Dan

The Steely Dan File

ideology- *Morph The Cat* 's release rectified any misunderstanding that Fagen may be a spent force. Coinciding with the release of Fagen's 3rd solo album was, for the first time, a nationwide tour of Donald Fagen as a solo act. Armed with a tight backup band Fagen opened to critical rave with a flurry of concerts in the cold northeast in March of 2006.

While many of the shows were sold out, or close to sold out, Fagen had a habit of ending the shows early (i.e. with no encore) if things didn't particularly sound right. Several shows clocked in well under 2 hours and caused irate fans to post their displeasure on many of the Steely Dan message boards that adorned the Internet. Add to the fact that for some reason Fagen refused to play any material from his 1993 solo disc *Kamakiriad* and you had the makings of a mini- rebellion in the world of Dandom.

Eventually the tour made it to the west coast and despite disappointing sales of the new disc Fagen's live performances were in fine form. San Francisco Chronicle critic Joel Selvin was mesmerized by Fagen's Oakland performance, declaring, "the scrupulous consistency of the set offered one glistening groove after another, each artfully decorated

Back to 'Nature

and meticulously arranged"[98]. Critic Ed Kane noted about Fagen's Los Angeles concert that, "Fagen came across very well as a performer and displayed a keen insight into entertaining his audience"[99]. Kane also noted however that, "the most surprising thing about the set list was how little material from *Morph* was presented." On most nights throughout his first ever-solo tour Fagen would play only two songs from his new release.

Perhaps another part of the reason for the poor cd sales for his new album stemmed from the whirlwind of confusion that engulfed the Steely Dan world when news of Fagen's new cd first surfaced in January. Apparently not consulting their astrologers Fagen and Becker were apparently still keen on making things up as they went along,
First it was announced that Fagen had a brand new studio album for release; *then* it was announced that he was undertaking a US tour. Before that information had properly sunk in, word came from Walter Becker's

---

[98] 'No static at all - Donald Fagen's sound as sleek as it's ever been' SF Chronicle Mar.30, 2006

[99] 'Donald Fagen in Los Angeles' by Edward Kane at jazz-review.com

The Steely Dan File

camp that he *too* was going to issue a new studio album; recording of it was well underway at studios in New York, several top jazz players were known to be taking part. And just as Fagen's shows were getting underway news hit the internet that Steely Dan, the *band*, would be undertaking an extensive US tour in the summer of 2006.....sharing a double-bill with none other than old 'Dan alumni Mike McDonald!

It was an information overload that in many ways was a replay of 1993 when news of Steely Dan's re-formation had begun. As had happened with Fagen's 1993 return to the music scene, things seemed to be transpiring in a haphazard and unproductive manner.

As had happened 13 years earlier Fagen came out with a solo disc. As had happened 13 years earlier news of Fagen's new music was eclipsed by word of a *Steely Dan* reunion....and as had happened a decade or so before Walter Becker was to come out with a solo album, that in all probability may have limited appeal. Becker's record company made such a blunder with the release of his first solo disc that they made sure it hit the record shops in late September of '94.....about two weeks *after* the Citizen Steely Dan tour ended.

Back to 'Nature

Similar patterns emerged in 2006 as it would take the better part of six weeks for Warner Brothers pr men to get Fagen's lead single "The H-Gang" on to a playlist in the New York area; right *after* his tour had concluded. By the time the summer Steely Dan/Mike McDonald tour had started Warner Brothers and Fagen had apparently given up on *Morph* – no big publicity to re-ignite interest- no *Morph* songs to be performed during the new tour. With the exception of the contemporary jazz world- *Morph The Cat* had vanished from the pop scene just a few months after it's promising release.

In the years ahead though, it is quite probable that *Morph The Cat* will age like the early Steely Dan release *Countdown To Ecstasy.* Like *Morph, Countdown* spent but 3 weeks in the US Top 40, but is now remembered as a shining example of how good American progressive rock can sound. *Morph* may have a similar fate- and the final chapter on its legacy remains to be written.

Becker and Fagen are perhaps oblivious to the current state of their standing in the annals of pop, rock and jazz music. Even with a trend of diminishing sales they can rest assured that their legacy as unique songwriters and performers is secure.

The Steely Dan File

Wheel Turning 'Round and Round

They came to the music industry as cocky young smart alecks and succeeded beyond their expectations in several areas. In the '70's they were seen as great songwriters of a new type of American standard- with an ability to weave several different music styles into the confines of their 5 minute tracks. They were seen as intelligent counter-culture icons that had a managed to buck the corporate arena rock system and still have a platinum album. Their appreciation of distinct elements of jazz and popular songs enabled them to break down radio racial barriers over the course of the entire decade....from the Latin flavor of "Do It Again" to the sophisticated funk of "Black Cow" and "FM" Steely Dan was an enigmatic sound that opened the ears of many to elements of musical heritages they many may never have heard before.

As they disappeared for the better part of a decade the public was able to digest their 1970's catalogue more properly over the years of 1983-1993. Their few punctures on the 1980's scene were subtle yet charming. While Becker tossed up an elegant polished pop with China Crisis, Fagen blessed

Back to 'Nature

us with an almost bossa nova style production in the semi-autobiographical *The Nightfly*.

Through fate and fans they were brought back together in an unrehearsed Steely Dan reunion that saw them following closely in the tradition of the rock n soul songs of their youth. Steely Dan songs long dormant to live performance were now rearranged for public listening not too unlike the jazzy and fake-jazzy sounds of the Brill Building icons. New material was more personal- still perfect from an audiologist perspective.

While the new 21st Century 'Dan may never be able to rise up to it's 20th Century cousins, it nevertheless is enjoyable and perhaps something more organic than any of the 1970's ear candy can ever be.

As the titanic Steely Dan continues it's way through the sea of musical turmoil during the summer of '07, there's something reassuring in their continued presence in the pop world. Steely Dan..the thinking man's rock band..Dan Steele..the unlikeliest supergroup...Outre Daniel..Hall of Famers and Grammy Winners.....Mr. Steely Dan.........it's still growing!

The Steely Dan File

Steely Dan/Donald Fagen 2003-2006 Releases
Everything Must Go (June 2003)
Somewhat of a polar opposite to 'Nature this 2003 set had warmer analogue feel to it. Recorded in New York both before and after 9/11 Everything Must Go was wiggy, funky and almost a real Blue Note release- it featured noted Blue Note pianist Bill Charlap on many tracks. From the Sienfeld-esque 'Blues Beach' to the Woody Allen-esque 'Lunch with Gina', EMG, continued the Steely saga in style. The title track was a haunting groove that featured some Coltrane influenced sax parts from Walt Weiskopf.

1 2 3 4 5 6 7 **8** 9 10

Morph The Cat (March 2006)
The third epic in Fagen's solo journey, Morph The Cat, seemed to crystallize Fagen's somber post 9/11 New York mood. Fed up with the terrorists and the Bush regime Fagen was able to articulate his feistiness in songs that grooved along in just the right time. The title track brought to life a New York City frozen in time…by inertia, circumstance…and fate.

1 2 3 4 5 6 7 **8.5** 9 10

The Steely Dan File

Steely Dan Appendixes

5

Discography
Chronology
Bibliography

The Steely Dan File

LP's & CD's

Date	Title	Label	Chart	RIAA
Oct. 1972	Can't Buy A Thrill	ABC x 758	7*	Platinum
July 1973	Countdown To Ecstasy	ABC x779	24**	Gold
March 1974	Pretzel Logic	ABC d808	8+	Platinum
April 1975	Katy Lied	ABC 846	13+	Platinum
April 1976	The Royal Scam	ABC d 931	15+	Platinum
September 1977	Aja	ABC 1006	3+	Platinum
April 1978	FM (Original soundtrack) [3 tracks]	MCA 12000/2	5+	Platinum
November 1978	Steely Dan /Greatest Hits	ABC 1107/2	30+	Platinum
November 1980	Gaucho	MCA 6102	9+	Platinum
June 1982	Gold	MCA10387	115	
Dec 1993	Citizen	MCA10981	-	Gold
May 1985	Decade	MCA11553	50	Platinum
November 1995	Alive In America	Giant24634	40+	
February 2000	Two Against Nature	Giant24719	6+	Platinum
August 2001	Show Biz Kids	MCA112407	-	-
June 2003	Everything Must Go	Reprise 48435	10+	Gold

*- Record World **-Cashbox +-Billboard

Steely Dan Appendixes

The Steely Dan Singles

Date	Title	Catalogue #	Chart
3/72	**Dallas** /Sail the Waterway	ABC 11323	-
11/18/72	**Do It Again**(edited)/Fire In Hole	ABC 11338	1 *
3/10/73	**Reelin' In The Years**/Only A Fool	ABC 11352	1 *
7/27/73	**Show Biz Kids**(edited)/Razor Boy	ABC 11382	9 *
10/20/73	**My Old School(edited)**/Pearl of the Quarter	ABC 11396	56 +
4/26/74	**Rikki Dont't Lose That Number**/ Any Major Dude	ABC 11439	2 *
9/20/74	**Pretzel Logic**/Through With Buzz	ABC 12033	59 #
5/17/75	**Black Friday**/Throw Back The Little Ones	ABC 12101	31 +
8/23/75	**Bad Sneakers**/Chain Lightning	ABC 12128	90 +
5/24/76	**Kid Charlemagne**/Green Earrings	ABC 12165	82 #
10/3/76	**The Fez**/Sign In Stranger	ABC 12222	59 #
1/2/77	**Haitian Divorce**/Sign In Stranger	ABC Anchor4152	17 **
11/19/77	**Peg**/I Got The News	ABC 12320	8 +

The Steely Dan File

4/1/78	**Deacon Blues**(edited)/Home At Last	ABC 12355	17 #
5/27/78	**FM** (No Static At All)(edited)/FM Reprise	MCA 40894	22 #
8/26/78	**Josie**/Black Cow	ABC 12404	26 +/#
11/22/80	**Hey Nineteen (edited)**/Bodhisattva (live)	MCA 51036	10 +/#
3/14/81	**Time Out Of Mind**/Bodhisattva (live)	MCA 51082	13 ##
6/8/81	**Babylon Sisters(edited)**/3rd World Man	MCA 51121	2 ***
02/28/00	**Cousin Dupree**	Giant 4265	30
9/01/00	**Jack of Speed (radio edit)**	Giant100158	8 ++
06/07/03	**Blues Beach**	Reprise	17#

Chart Position Sources:

*= Record World +=Cashbox #=Billboard
##=Billboard Rock Tracks **=BBC World Service
***=Harmony Illustrated Encyclopedia of Rock ++= CMJ Radio Chart

Steely Dan Appendixes

Donald Fagen Solo Albums

Date	Title	Cat. #	PK	RIAA
October 1982	The Nightfly	Warner 23696	11	Gold
1991	Live At The Beacon-w/NY Rock 'n Soul Revue	Giant 24423	187	---
May 1993	Kamakiriad	Reprise 45230	3**	Platinum
March 2006	Morph The Cat	Reprise 45570	26	

Donald Fagen Solo Hits

Date Issued	Title	Cat.#	Highest Chart #
10/16/82	IGY (What A Beautiful World)	Warner 29900	17 +
1/6/83	New Frontier(edited)	Warner 29792	80 #
3/26/88	Century's End	Warner 27972	13 ##
11/2/91	Pretzel Logic	Giant 5180	17 ##
6/5/93	Tomorrow's Girls	Reprise 18502	20 ##
2/2006	H-Gang	Reprise101704	-
6/2006	What I Do	Reprise 101796	-

+-Cashbox #-Billboard Hot 100 ##-Billboard Rock Tracks

The Steely Dan File

Walter Becker Discography

Date	Title/Artist	Label	
1985	Flaunt The Imperfection/China Crisis	Warner 25296	Producer/guitarist
1987	Light & Shade/Fra Lippo Lippi	Virgin	producer
1989	Diary of a Hollow Horse/China Crisis	A&M/Virgin 5225	producer
1990	Flying Cowboys/Rickie Lee Jones	Geffen 24246	Producer/writer
1991	Blue Pacific/Michael Franks	Reprise	Producer (3songs)
1993	Kamakiriad/Donald Fagen	Reprise	Producer/guitarist
1993	The Lost Tribe/The Lost Tribe	Windham Hill	producer
1994	Eleven Tracks of Whack	Giant 22609	Solo album (vocals/guitar)

Steely Dan Appendixes

Promotional Items/ Imports/ Rarities

Year	Title	Catalogue
1969	Alias Boona/Terence Boylan	MGM/Verve FTS 3070
1971	Barbara Joan Streisand	Columbia 564459
1971	Come Back Baby	Peer Southern acetate
1971	You Gotta Walk It, Like You talk It (soundtrack)......	Spark 02
1972	Dallas/Sail the Waterway	ABC 11323
1972	Dallas (promo)	Probe 562
1972	Reunion/John Henry Kurtz	ABC x742s

The Steely Dan File

	(featuring Hodder, Baxter, Gordon)	
1972	Rootin'/Narasota(featuring Baxter, Fagen)	ABC x757
1972	Do It Again (edited)	Probe/Pathé Marconi(2C006-94048)
1972	Do It Again	PROBE/Phonogram Greece PRO 505
1972	Do it again (edited)	PROBE 3C 000 60032(Italy)
1972	Do It Again (edited)	Probe 577
1972	Do It Again/Fire In the Hole	EMI/Electrola
1973	Reelin In the years	Probe 587
1973	Do It Again	Probe 89103 (Ecuador)
1973	Do It Again (edited)	Probe Japan

1973	Dirty Work/ Only A Fool Would Say That	Probe HollandC 006-94048
1973	Countdown To Ecstasty (Asia)	Probe 8050
1973	Countdown To Ecstasy (Jukebox EP)	ABC Ilp 225
1973	My Old School (edited)	Probe 606 (UK)
1973	Bodhisattva (edited)/Razor Boy	Probe (Asia only)
1973	Show Biz Kids/Razor Boy	Probe 4C006

Steely Dan Appendixes

		94698(Belgium)
1973	Can't Buy A Thrill (Taiwan)	Liming 2543
1973	Thomas Jefferson Kaye	Dunhill Records #DSX-50149
1974	Pretzel Logic (Jukebox EP Quad)	ABCllpq 255
1974	Can't Buy A Thrill (quadraphonic)	ABC Command 40009
1974	Countdown To Ecstasy (quadraphonic)	ABC Command 40010
1974	East St.Louis Toodle-oo	ABC spdj 20 (7 inch 33 rpm)
1974:	First Grade /Thomas Jefferson Kaye	ABC Dunhill 50142
1974	Pretzel Logic (quad)	ABC Command 40015
1974	Rikki Don't Lose That Number	Probe Label 1C006 95438(German)
1974	Rikki Don't Lose That Number	Probe 5C006 95438 (Holland)
1974	Can't Buy A Thrill (different cover)	Probe Singapore
1974	Rikki Don't Lose That Number	Probe IPR-10543
1975	Black Friday/Throw Back..	Electrola/ABC
1975	Black Friday/(mono)	ABC wl 12101
1975	Katy Lied (Asian issue)	Probe/Toshiba

The Steely Dan File

		80181
1975	Pretzel Logic/Rikki	ABC 2731
1975	Bad Sneakers/(mono)	ABCwl 12128
1976	Viernes Negro (1976 Spanish "Black Friday")	ABC SG-0012
1976	The Royal Scam (Japan)	Nippon Columbia 8028
1976	Kid Charlemagne/Green Earring	ABC SG 0032 (Spain)
1976	Haitian divorce/Sign in stranger	ABC 17612 (German)
1976	Kid Charlemagne/Green Earrings	ABC-17-095 (German)
1976	The Royal Scam	ABC - 68011 (French)
1977	Four Tracks from Steely Dan	Anchor 12003
1977	Can't Buy A Thrill (gold vinyl)	Dunhill 9022 (Canada)
1977	Aja (Japanese)	Nippon ColumbiaYX-8114-AB
1977	Aja/Aja (mono)	ABC spdj 33
1977	Aja (reel to reel)	ABC 6716
1977	Peg/I Got The News	ABC 45-099 (asia)
1977	Terrence Boylan (featuring Fagen)	Asylum 7E 1091
1977	Indian Summer/Poco (featuring Fagen)	ABC ab989
1978	Deacon Blues/Home At last	ABCTDS-005 (aus)

Steely Dan Appendixes

1978	Mannequin(soundtrack)/Marc Jordan (featuring Fagen)	Warner 3143
1978	Deacon Blues/Josie	ABC spdj 35
1978	Deacon Blues/Josie	ABC4217 (UK)
1978	You Gotta Walk It ...	JEM 7005
1978	Do It Again/Reelin' In The Years	ABC 02.1344(Spain)
1978	Steely Dan (compilation)	ABC Japan 8140
1978	Kid Charlemagne/Western World	MCA MCS-10893,(NZ)
1978	Rikki Don't Lose ...	ABC UK 4241
1978	Josie/Josie (mono)	ABC spdj 45
1978	Aja (red vinyl)	ABC 9022
1978	Katy Lied (original master)	MFSL 1-014
1978	Here At The Western World	ABC spdj 47
1979	Flying Home/Summer(featuring Denny Dias)	(Touchstone BBT113T).
1979	Aja (Argentina)	Music hall 50.16.046.) mono
1979	1972-1978 (compilation)	ABC Portugal 1107
1979	Very Best Of	MCA 4027
1979	Greatest Hits (w/o Do It Again)	EMI/Ole Korea 275
1980	Hey Nineteen	MCA promo cassette single
1980	Gaucho (Japan)	MCA/Victor6 243

The Steely Dan File

1980	Gaucho (Italy)	MCA4114
1980	Hey Nineteen/Bodhisattva	MCA 102677(Spain)
1980	Hey Nineteen (Japan)	VIMX-1514
1980	Gaucho (Japanese)	VIM-6243
1981	Gaucho (remastered)	MCA 16009
1981	The Early Years (demo recordings)	Aero 040
1981	Babylon Sisters/(mono)	MCA 51121
1981	Gaucho (RARE COVER)	MCA KOREAN:#889
1981	Do It Again/Rikki	MCA 696 018 (Brazil)
1981	Steely Dan (Compilation)	VIM-4076~7
1982	Reeling in The years (EP)	MCA 852 (UK) (12 inch 45 rpm)
1982	FM/East St.Louis Toodle-oo	MCA 786 (UK)
1982	Do It Again (lp version)	MCA OG-9321 (UK)
1982	Gold (with EP)	MCF3145
1985	Very Best Of (double lp)	MCA TVT DNL 1 (UK)

1986	Sun Mountain	SHLP128 (UK) (lp)
1986	Berry Town	Bell 23007
1987	Do It Again (lp)	Telstar 2624 (UK) (lp)
1988	Stone Piano	THBL054(CD)
1992	Sun Mountain	TB 139 (CD)
1992	Do It Again	MCA 54310
1993	You Gotta Walk It...	SFM357 (CD)
1993	Remastered-The Best	MCA10967 (CD)

Steely Dan Appendixes

	Steely Dan	
1993	Interview	MCA Press Kit
1993	Remastered-4 track sampler	WMCD-10967
1994	Reeling In The Years	MCA UK CD single
1995	Fagen and Becker Sampler	MCA sd101
1996	Reeling In The Years (live)	Giant CD ep single
1997	Gaucho (DTS mix)	DTS1014
1998	Aja	SVLP0030
1999	Cousin Dupree/edit	Giant 4265
2000	Sampler	CATR05001-2
2000	Words and Music	Giant 4281
2000	What A Shame About Me	Giant 4267
2000	Jack of Speed	Giant 100158
2000	Two Against Nature	BMG/Giant (Asian pressing) BVCG-21003
2000	Two Against Nature	Giant /WEA(Japanese Pressing) BVCG-21003
2000	Two Against Nature	Reprise 62190 Germany (lp)
2000	Two Against Nature (DVD-A)	WEA24719
2001	Janie Runaway	Reprise 100342 promo
2001	Lexicon presents….	Pro-100029
2003	Things I Miss the Most	Reprise101154
2003	One hour Sale	Reprise 101112 promo
2003	Blues Beach/Last Mall	Reprise US/Japan promo
2003	Papersleeve Box Set	MCA Victor MVCZ-10072/3/4/5/6/7 and UICY-3094

The Steely Dan File

2003	Blues Beach	Reprise 101108
2003	Confessions (DVD)	PRO-DVD-101114)
2003	Everything Must Go (DVD-A)	Warner48435
2003	Everything Must Go (HDCD)	Warner(China only) 2 cd set
2003	Gaucho (SACD)	Geffen73802
2003	Kamakiriad (DVD-A)	R9-73782
2004	Everything Must Go (vinyl)	Reprise9362-48435-1
2004	Gaucho (DVD-A)	MCA 176719
2004	Do It Again (Saint Vincent's vocal mix)/(dubstrumental)	Wax Jackers (12 inch club mix)
2004	Time Out of Mind	Wax Jackers (12 inch club mix)
2005	Aja (12x12 sleeve)	Geffen UICY-95016
2005	3 Originals	Universal 3803352
2005	3 Originals (Vol.2)	Universal 1321762
2006	Morph The Cat (DVD Audio)	Reprise 49976
2006	Definitive Collection	Geffen/UMG 675202
2006	Definitive Collection (Japan)	UICY-1386
2007	Millenium Collection	Geffen 364K6
2007	Aja	SVLP0030
2007	The Nightfly Trilogy (MVI)	Reprise M06SVS

A Steely Dan Chronology

1967-Donald Fagen meets Walter Becker at Bard College in Annandale-On-The Hudson in upstate New York. Fagen, a native of Passaic, New Jersey, has been playing piano since childhood. Walter Becker, born in Westchester, but raised in Queens, learned guitar by himself and from his friend Randy California, future leader of the band Spirit.

1969- Becker and Fagen join Jay & The Americans touring ensemble as bass player and keyboardist,,respectively, and cut demo tapes under the supervision of Kenny Vance. These demo tapes later surface on the albums, 'The Early Years' (1981) and 'Sun Mountain, (1986).

The Steely Dan File

Fagen and Becker both appear on the album 'Alias Boona' (MGM) by Terence Boylan, their friend from Bard College.

Becker and Fagen do horn arrangements on 'There Goes My Baby' the last hit single issued by Jay & the Americans.

1970- Future Steely Dan guitarist Denny Dias recruits Fagen and Becker for his Long Island based band Demian. They record demos with vocalist Keith Thomas, that later surface on the *Sun Mountain* lp.

Becker, Fagen and Dias record as 'The Original Soundtrack' for the film 'You Gotta Walk It Like You Talk It' (Spark) with help from John Discepello on drums and Kenny Vance and Marty Kupersmith on vocals (all three members of Jay and the Americans back up band.)

Barbra Streisand records the Becker/Fagen song 'I Mean To Shine' with Fagen on keyboards. The song appears on the 1971 Epic album *Barbara Joan Streisand*.

Through Kenny Vance Fagen and Becker meet producer Gary Kannon" Katz, the producer of the Boston based group Bead Game (Epic).

Steely Dan File Appendixes

1971- Fagen and Becker record demos with Dias, Elliot Randall (guitar), Keith Thomas (vocals) and John Mazzi (drums) which surface in 1985 on 'The Old Regime' (Thunderbolt).

The idea of forming "steely dan" is born during recording sessions for a fledgling female singer, Linda Hoover, whom Fagen and Becker have written songs. Session guitarist Jeff "Skunk" Baxter, ex-Ultimate Spinach guitarist, meets Fagen and Becker after being brought in to the sessions by Gary Katz. Although Katz produced the album for MGM Records it was never issued.

Katz is hired by ABC Dunhill in Los Angeles and gets Fagen and Becker jobs as staff songwriters. Katz produces the band Narasota with help from Becker and Fagen and enlists engineer Roger Nichols to work of the first Steely Dan sessions.

With approval from ABC Dunhill executive Steve Barri Steely Dan is formed as Becker and Fagen begin recording with studio musicians Jeff Baxter and Victor Feldman. The song 'Everyone's Gone To The Movies' is the first Steely Dan track copyrighted and recorded, Donald Fagen sings lead vocals and gets back up support from Flo and Eddie.

The Steely Dan File

1972- Former Mommas & Poppas lead singer Denny Doherty records two tracks with Becker, Fagen and Nichols, 'Sail The Waterway' and 'Giles of the River'.

Baxter and drummer Jim Hodder record on the album *Reunion* by John Henry Kurtz.

Steely Dan issues their first single, 'Dallas' with the lineup of Becker (bass), Baxter (pedal steel guitar), Fagen (keyboards), Feldman (Percussion) and ex-Bead Game member Jim Hodder (drums and lead vocals). After being issued in March the single is quickly withdrawn by ABC Dunhill and is never re-issued.

Fagen and Baxter record on the album *Rootin'* by Narasota. Becker and Fagen compose one song for the album, *Canyon Ladies*.

ABC executives give the green light for Steely Dan to record a full album. Becker calls guitarist Denny Dias to join the group. The original Steely Dan of Becker, Fagen, Baxter, Dias and Hodder begin recording 'Can't Buy A Thrill' in June at the Village Recorder studios in West Hollywood.

With the album nearing completion ABC executives inform the group that they are lining up a series of venues for them to perform at.

Steely Dan File Appendixes

Although he is the bands lead singer, Fagen decides he can't be the groups frontman in concert. Katz recruits New Jersey native David Palmer to be the bands new lead singer.

'Can't Buy A Thrill' is issued by ABC Records in September. Becoming popular with FM dj's it quickly gets airplay and debuts at #149 on the US charts (Cashbox) on October 21.

Steely Dan makes its' live debut at a small club in Pasadena, CA in September.

Steely Dan tour the US with fellow ABC Records act, The James Gang and makes its' New York debut in early November at Max's Kansas City. The very first official concert given by Steely Dan is on October 1, 1972 in Seattle. One of their first big concerts is as the Opening act for top ABC Records star Jim Croce in Chicago.

In December Steely Dan opens for the Kinks on their US tour.

1973-Through their touring manager, Joel Cohen, Steely Dan are signed up to tour with fellow California acts, The Doobie Brothers and Loggins & Messina. In concert David Palmer handles all lead vocals despite having

The Steely Dan File

only done two songs as lead vocalist on the album.

In January the band records two television spots, one on 'American Bandstand' (ABC-TV) and the other on NBC-TV's 'Midnite Special'.

An edited version of *Can't Buy A Thrill* opening track 'Do It Again' climbs into the US Top 10 in February.

In April the band starts playing large venues (the Spectrum in Philadelphia, the Nassau Coliseum on Long Island etc.) along with The Doobie Brothers and Seals and Croft.

In the first of many personnel changes David Palmer is sacked as the groups' lead singer. Fagen now takes over as sole lead vocalist for the band as recording of a new album begins.

'Can't Buy A Thrill' becomes a Gold Record and hits #7 on the US lp chart (Record World). New single 'Reeling In The Years' (a drastically different sound from 'Do It Again') soars into the US Top 10 in May.

In July newly recorded 'Show Biz Kids' meets with resistance from AM Radio and fails to

Steely Dan File Appendixes

break US Top 30, much to the disappointment of the band. New lp,
Countdown To Ecstasy, likewise struggles on the chart and peaks at #35 on Billboard magazines lp chart.

1973-Despite a major tour the band finds its' popularity slipping. New single 'My Old School' fails to break the US Top 40 when it is issued in October.
The original Steely Dan makes it's last tv appearance by appearing on American Bandstand. They "perform", 'My Old School' and 'Bodhisattva'.

ABC Records pushes the band to record a new album and resume touring. New members Jeff Porcaro (drums) and Mike McDonald (piano and vocals) are added to the Steely Dan live ensemble for concerts in California.

1974- Steely Dan's first tour of England is cancelled in January due to the 'energy crisis'.

In March Steely Dan begin their last major tour in California and soon after play concerts up and down the eastcoast.

'Pretzel Logic' beomes the groups second Gold album and hits #8 on Billboard's lp chart. Lead single, 'Rikki Don't Lose That

The Steely Dan File

Number', becomes a monster hit, hitting US #2 (Record World).

In May Steely Dan play their first gigs in England to enthusiastic crowds. Record sales however remain slow in Britain and 'Rikki...' fails to chart at all on the BBC chart.

Upon returning from the UK Steely Dan continue touring in Canada and California and finish up their tour on July 5th in Santa Monica. One month later it is announced that Jeff Baxter and Jimmy Hodder are out of the band.

In virtual seclusion Fagen and Becker conduct recording sessions for their new album at ABC Recording studios. Top name session players like Hal Blaine, Michael Omartian and Larry Carlton take part in addition to remaining members Dias, Porcaro and McDonald. Becker now handles guitar chores in addition to his bass playing.

1975-During final mixing of their new album *'Katy Lied'*, Steely Dan are incensed when a faulty noise reduction system damages the master tapes.

'Katy Lied' is released in May and sells moderately well despite of the bands lack of visibilty. Fagen and Becker perform no con-

Steely Dan File Appendixes

certs in 1975 and conduct no major interviews. In a publicity photo Steely Dan are presented as a quartet of Becker, Fagen, Dias and Porcaro.

'Black Friday' becomes the bands 4th Top 40 hit on Billboards chart peaking at #37. Follow up single 'Bad Sneakers' bombs however, becoming Steely Dan's first single since 1972's 'Dallas' to fail to chart at all.

1976-Steely Dan returns with the powerful album 'The *Royal Scam*' and does major interviews with 'Music Gig' magazine and Melody Maker in London.

'The Royal Scam' becomes the bands 4th Gold album in the US and their biggest yet in the UK hitting #11 on the BBC chart.

New sessions begin with an all-star cast of, among others: sax player Tom Scott, drummer Steve Gadd, pianist Joe Sample and bassist Chuck Rainey.

1977-'Hatian Divorce' becomes Steely Dan's only Top 20 hit in the UK, peaking at #17 on the BBC chart.

In July Fagen and Becker appear on an LA radio station and debut new song 'Black

The Steely Dan File

Cow'. Plans for a autumn tour are cancelled after one rehearsal.

Much anticipated new album 'Aja' is released in October and soars up the chart. It is certified Gold within 1 week and hits #3 on Billboard.

In an interview with Rolling Stone's Cameron Crowe (in December) Fagen and Becker announce that they have signed a new contract with Warner Brothers Records.

1978-'Peg', from the '*Aja*' album, becomes Steely Dan's first Top 20 hit in 4 years and peaks at #11 in Billboard (it hits #8 on Cashbox's chart).

Five-year old album *'Countdown To Ecstasy'* begins to sell again and is certified Gold by the RIAA in April.

Through a mutual friend, Dick Lapalm, Steely Dan collaborate with jazz great Woody Herman on an album in Los Angeles. The Concorde release, 'Chick, Donald, Walter and Woodrow' is a popular jazz album when it is issued in the summer.

With Jeff Porcaro on drums Steely Dan record the track 'FM (No Static At All)' for MCA Re-

Steely Dan File Appendixes

cords. It is the title song to a film about an LA radio station.

At the annual Grammy Awards ceremony Steely Dan wins for Best Engineered Album (non-classical) but loses the Album of the Year award to the Eagles 'Hotel California'.

'Deacon Blues' follows 'Peg' into the US Top 20 in June and is quickly followed on the charts by an edited version of 'FM', which peaks at #22. The 'FM' album meanwhile goes Platinum and hits US #5.

In their first work for Warner Brothers Records Fagen and Becker produce the jazz album 'Apogee' by the Pete Christlieb/Warne Marshe Quintet.

A third single from 'Aja', 'Josie' becomes the 4th Top 40 hit for Steely Dan in 1978 in September and helps propel new compilation 'Steely Dan/Greatest Hits' to Platinum status (for 1,000,000 copies sold).

1979-MCA Records buys Steely Dan's record label (ABC Records) and begins re-releasing all of Steely Dan's albums, all of which are now certified as Gold or Platinum disks.

The Steely Dan File

Fagen and Becker both relocate to New York City and begin recording a new album for Warner Brothers.

Steely Dan is voted 'Band of the Decade' in the decade ending issue of Musian, Player and Listener magazine.

1980-Amid much legal and personal difficulties Steely Dan record their 7th album, '*Gaucho*' in New York and L.A. After some legal wrangling MCA Records releases the disk in December and Becker and Fagen are now free from their contractual obligations to the label.

Lead single, 'Hey 19', enters the US Top 40 upon its' release in December, eventually hitting #10.

1981-Brilliant single 'Time Out of Mind' is Steely Dan's swan song and hits #22 in Billboard's op 40 in April, soon after Fagen announces that Steely Dan has been dissolved.

'Babylon Sisters' is released as the final Steely Dan single in June by MCA Records but fails to chart on Billboard or Cashbox.

Fagen begins work on a solo album for Warner Brothers and records a song for the

Steely Dan File Appendixes

animated film Heavy Metal, 'True Companion'.

1982-MCA Records release a compilation of Steely Dan tracks called '*Gold*' and in England releases an ep featuring 'FM' and 'East St.Louis Toodle oo'.

Donald Fagen's solo album, 'The Nightfly' is released in October and is very popular with fans and critics. It hits #11 on Billboard's lp chart and is certified Gold. Two hit singles emerge, 'IGY (What A Beautiful World)' and 'The New Frontier'.

1984-On assignment for Warner Brothers Records Walter Becker flies to England to produce 'Flaunt The Imperfection' for China Crisis.

1985-China Crisis' album hits #9 on the UK charts and spawns three Top 20 hits. The band tours the US to sell out crowds and the album chart briefly on Billboard and is popular on "new wave' radio stations.

1986-Both Fagen and Becker take part in the Gary Katz produced sessions for new singer Rosie Vela on A&M records.

1988-After cancelling the release of his second solo album Fagen does soundtrack work

The Steely Dan File

for the film 'Bright Lights, Big City'. Both the film and the soundtrack are only mildly successful upon release.

1989-Walter Becker and engineer Roger Nichols team up and produce two albums. One with Rickie Lee Jones and one with China Crisis. Jones's album puts her back on the US charts while the China Crisis album bombs causing them to be dropped from their UK label Virgin.

In a concert to honor famed Brill Building composers Bert Burns and Jerry Ragavoy Donald Fagen performs live for the first time in 15 years in September at a small club in New York.

1990-Along with 'The New York Rock and Soul Revue' Donald Fagen plays a headlining concert at the Beacon Theater in New York in April.

1991-In June Becker and Fagen decide to team up again and work on Fagen's solo disc for Warner Brothers. Becker will produce and help out on guitar and bass and Roger Nichols will over see the digital production.

Fagen leads a major concert of the New York Rock and Soul Revue at the Beacon Theater that will be recorded and eventually issued

Steely Dan File Appendixes

on Giant Records. Several Steely Dan songs are played including 'Pretzel Logic' and 'Chain Lightning'. After the concerts Fagen is interviewed by the CNN cable TV station.

1992-As work on Fagen's new album continues in New York and Hawaii (where Becker has his own recording studio) another New York Rock and Soul Revue tour is undertaken. Becker even joins on this tour as more Steely Dan songs are added to the playlist.

'Live At The Beacon', an album of material culled from the 1991 New York concerts is released by the New York Rock and Soul Revue and charts briefly on the Billboard lp chart. 'Pretzel Logic' by Fagen and Mike McDonald hits #17 on Billboard's Rock Tracks Top 40.

1993-In May Fagen's new solo disc, *'Kamakiriad'*, is issued by the Warner distributed Reprise Records and debuts at #10 on Billboard's lp chart. In July *'Kamakiriad'* hits #3 on Cashbox's lp chart and is eventually certified Platinum.

Fresh on the success of 'Kama*kiriad*' Fagen and Becker decide to re-group Steely Dan and a major US tour is initiated in Detroit in August. Almost the entire tour is sold out with high points being an August 24 sold out

The Steely Dan File

Madison Square Garden performance and a sold out Hollywood concert that featured Denny Dias as a guest guitarist.

In December MCA Records issues a definitve box set called *'Citizen Steely Dan'* that includes a booklet of rare pictures and memorablia from the early '70's tours.

1994-Becker is signed by Giant Records to cut his own solo album. Fagen flies to Hawaii to help out on production and keyboard work.

In April Steely Dan begin what amounts to their first world tour. Sold out concerts are played by the 'Steely Dan Orchestra' in Tokyo, St.Petersburg, Florida, San Francisco, London and Dublin. Many of the shows are recorded and are released as bootleg cd's.

Walter Becker's debut solo album *'Eleven Tracks of Whack'* is released in September to critical praise. Becker conducts an extended interview with the PBS tv network and performs some of the album during Steely Dan 'Citizen Dan' tour in September and October'.

1995-Culled from the previous two years of touring the Donald Fagen produced *'Alive In America'* returns Steely Dan to the US charts upon its' release in October. *'Alive In Amer-*

Steely Dan File Appendixes

ica' hits #40 on Billboards lp chart becoming Steely Dan's 9th Top 40 lp.

In the midst of a brief promotional tour in New York City Steely Dan play live on CBS-tv's Late Night with David Letterman; their first tv Âappearance in 21 years.

1996-Steely Dan undertake the 'Art Crimes' tour in the US to sold out crowds. With Becker now helping out on vocals early Steely Dan classics like 'Midnite Cruiser' and 'Do It Again' are added to the set list. At a California gig Boz Scaggs joins for a 10 minute version of 'My Old School'.

1997-Fagen and Becker delve into work on a new Steely Dan album in New York amid much secrecy.

Becker oversees an official, but very humorous, Steely Dan website at www.steelydan.com.

1998-As the new Steely Dan album nears completion at New York City sessions Fagen and Becker do a brief interview on a Seattle FM radio station. Fagen indicates that the album is tentatively set for spring 1999 release and might be followed by a summer tour.

The Steely Dan File

Long neglected by the mainstream rock world Steely Dan are nominated for membership in the Rock 'n Roll Hall of Fame in Cleveland.

1999-Fagen and Becker finish up work on the new Steely Dan album with studio musicians and the permanent Steely Dan ensemble. Notable guest musicians include sax man Chris Potter and new 'Dan guitarists John Herington.

A documentary on the recording of *Aja* is released on video and DVD. It was originally a part of the UK series 'The Greatest Albums in Rock History'.

1999-Radio station KFOG in San Francisco debuts 'Cousin Dupree' from the forthcoming album on December 24, 1999.

2000- Steely Dan's new album, their 8th studio release, *Two Against Nature* is released in the US on February 28 on Giant Records. In the US the album is distributed by Warner Brothers, but overseas it is released under BMG.

Steely Dan launch a world tour with a concert in New York City. This concert is taped for a television special on PBS in the US. It is later issued as a video and DVD.

Steely Dan File Appendixes

Fagen and Becker receive the prestigous Founders Award from ASCAP.

Two Against Nature hits #6 on the Billboard lp chart and becomes a Platinum album for 1,000,000 copies sold in the US.

'Jack of Speed' becomes a Top 10 hit on the CMJ radio chart in the US.

After many years of neglect Steely Dan are selected for induction into the Rock 'n Roll Museum in Cleveland, Ohio.

2001- At the 43rd Annual Grammy Award presentation Steely Dan steal the show by winning four Grammy Awards. Among the awards won are those for Best Engineered Recording and the much-coveted Album of the Year award.

Fagen and Becker perform at the Rock 'n Roll Hall of Fame ceremonies in March.

The prestigous Berklee School of Music bestow Fagen and Becker with Honorary Doctorates at their annual ceremonies.

Work begins on a new Steely Dan album in Hawaii. Fagens indicates that he may also record his 3rd solo album

The Steely Dan File

2003- 'Everything Must Go', a New York recorded set, is released by Reprise Records in June and debuts at #10 on Billboard's album chart.

Steely Dan undertakes a major US tour that ends in August in Hawaii.

2004- Steely Dan's longtime saxophonist, Cornelius Bumpus, dies of a heart attack.

Donald Fagen records new solo material in New York and launches a literary website of donaldfagen.com

2006- Donald Fagen undertakes his first ever tour as a solo artist. Essentially touring to promote his new album, *Morph The Cat*, Fagen performs with a band of first rate studio musicians across the continental US in February and March.

Morph The Cat, Fagen's third solo album is issued by Reprise Records in March. It debuts at #26, becoming the 14th Steely Dan related Top 40 Album in the US.

Walter Becker announces that he is recording his second solo album in New York.

Steely Dan File Appendixes

Fagen and Becker undertake a Steely Dan tour along with longtime associate Michael McDonald.

2007- Steely Dan undertakes a world tour giving concerts in the US, the UK, Europe, Japan, Australia and New Zealand

Donald Fagen releases a box-set of solo material, *The Nightfly Trilogy*. The 7 disc set includes Surround Sound mixes of each of Fagen's solo albums as well as a 10-track audio disc of rarities.

Press reports indicate work on a new Steely Dan album has begun.

The Steely Dan File

Steely Dan File Appendixes

A Selected Steely Dan Bibliography

1971
NY Times 9/20/71-
> `*Genial Put Down of Society' by AH Weiler* A review of the Peter Locke film You Gotta Walk It Like You Talk It. Donald Fagen's name is written as "Donald Fagin" in the film credits

1972
ABC Dunhill Records Press Release 9/72-
> A brief 2-page press release featuring quotes from Fagen, Becker and Baxter

The Steely Dan File

Pasadena Star News 9/21/72-
> Music critic Geoff Kelly, labels Steely Dan a "competent folk-oriented rock band" and notes their current gig at the club Ice House.

Salt Lake City Tribune 10/20/72 p.2C-
> Critic David Proctor claims Steely Dan's music is "plenty good enough".

Los Angeles Free Press 10/27/72-
> 'Rock & Roll via Third Stream' by Chris Van Ness. A detailed interview with Fagen and Becker

Variety 11/8/72-
> 'East Coast hard rock sextet is making waves' by Kirb, Steely Dan's first NY concert at Max's Kansas City is reviewed. The 45 'Do It Again' is also reviewed.

Pasadena Star News 11/17/72-
> Note Steely Dan's upcoming week long showcase at the Whiskey-A-Go-go

Rolling Stone 11/23/72 p.66.
> Critic James Isaacs gives Steely Dan's debut a disappointing review and cites them as "...an LA rock band that is headed by a pair of transplanted Gotham mavericks named Donald Fagen and Walter C. Becker" and that they're forte is "cha-cha-cha"

Good Times (NY)- 12/72.
> Music Critic Janis Cercone gives *Can't Buy A Thrill* a great review.

The Daily Review (Hayward,CA) 12/29/72 p.34-
> Steely Dan is called "Superstars of Tomorrow"

1973

Salt Lake City Tribune 1/29/73 p.9-
> 'Unfamiliar Performers Draw Crowd in SL". A review of a Steely Dan/Doobie Brothers concert. Makes note of Steely Dan playing much new material.

Steely Dan File Appendixes

Oakland Tribune 2/73 -
> Critic Peter Cowan declares that Steely Dan are "Rising from the wasteland, crisp exacting, produced in layers of pulsating sound."

Winnipeg Free Press 3/3/73 -
> The Rock Scene by Richie Yorke- Becker declares that *"Do It Again kind of recorded itself."*

Rolling Stone 4/23/73 p.20=
> 'Ultimate Spinach Meets Naked Lunch's Dildo' by Judith Sims. A brief interview with Fagen, Becker and Katz.

Winnipeg Free Press 6/9/73 p109
> The Rock Scene by Richie Yorke- In a detailed interview Fagen and Becker declare that their 1972 was "an educational experience...we'd never lived in a Holiday Inn for six weeks before."

Billboard 7/14/73-
> *Countdown To Ecstasy* is given an excellent review, Billboard cites them as " powerful new group".

Melody Maker 7/21/73-
> 'Steely Dan's Smart Rock. by Mark Plummer. Fagen and Becker give their first interview to the British press. Article features a picture of the original Steely Dan sextet.

Winona Sunday News 7/22/73 p5B
> Critic Steve Edstrom declares *Countdown To Ecstasy* is "well-produced, dancing rock and roll."

The Herald (Chicago) 8/3/73 p.37
> Playback by Tom Von Malder Steely Dan is "greater than the sum of its part"

Rolling Stone 8/16/73 p.34
> Critic David Logan gives *Countdown To Ecstasy* an excellent review.

Melody Maker 8/18/73 p.34-
> 'Countdown gets an ecstatic critique.

The Steely Dan File

Winnipeg Free Press 9/15/73 p.99
    Critic Andy Mellen states that *Countdown To Ecstasy is* "a noticable improvement over the groups first lp."

1974

Salinas Journal (Kansas) 2/3/74-
    'Different View From Steely Dan' by Richard Truba

The Valley news (Van Nuys) 3/8/74-
    'Steely Dan Returning to Glendale' by Vic Field

Tucson Daily Citizen 3/25/74 p.13-
    'Steely Dan brings crowd to its feet' by Larry Fleischman

Press-Telegram (Pasadena) 5/7/74 p18 –
    'Auditorium Fails to tarnish Steely Concert' by Denise Kusel

Rolling Stone 5/23/74 p.73-
    'Stainless Steely Band' by Bud Scoppa. High praise for *Pretzel Logic*, Scoppa claims they are 'one of America's best bands; surely one of the most original.'

Down Beat 5/23/74 p.18

Melody maker 5/25/74 p.34
    'Get Dan and get with it!' by Chris Welch. Rave reviews for Steely Dan's UK concerts.

Melody Maker 6/1/74 p.14-
    Steely Dan: MM Band Breakdown by C.Welch Each member of the original band is profiled and interviewed. Fagen talks about Nazi's and Becker talks about David Palmer's dismissal and Steely Dan's newest song \This Mobile Home' which they play at the conclusion of every concert.

Rolling Stone 8/15/74 p.32-
    'Steely Dan Comes Up Swinging- Number Five with a Dildo' by Charles Perry. Citing them as 'America's unlikeliest supergroup' Rolling Stone gives Steely Dan their biggest US press exposure to date.

Steely Dan File Appendixes

Pacific Stars & Stripes 8/25/74 p.17-
> Rock critic Tom Campbell, in noting the departure of Baxter and Hodder, states that "Steely Dan will continue as a trio."

Rolling Stone 8/29/74 p.32-
> article notes the ousting of Hodder and Baxter from the band and the band's break with manager Joel Cohen.

1975

Billboard 4/11/75 –
> Top Album Picks-*Katy Lied* is reviewed favorably as Billboard cites Steely Dan as "the premier American rock group to emerge in several years."

Melody Maker 4/26/75-
> A lukewarm review of *Katy Lied*

Rolling Stone 5/8/75-
> *Katy Lied* is ripped by Julian Mendolhson

Stereo Review 8/75 p.84-
> An excellent review for *Katy Lied*; reviewer notes ex-lead singer David Palmer's collaboration with Carole King.

Winnipeg Free Press 8/30/75 p34
> "…..Brother What a Band" by Cameron Crowe- A profile of the new Doobie Brothers lineup featuring Baxter and McDonald.

1976

Corpus Christie Times 5/14/76
> 'Here Are A Couple of Ideas…" by Dave Marsh Longtine 'Dan critic Marsh declares, "the excellent melodies that brought hit singles…is gone almost completely." He also declares that Fagen's voice is "close to becoming a major annoyance."

Rolling Stone 6/17/76 p.13
> 'Steely Dan: No Silly Love Songs Here' by Richard Cromelin. A generally condescending piece that features a spliced up publicity photo of Fagen and Becker labelling them 'ghoulish'.

The Steely Dan File

Melody Maker 6/17/76 –
'Art For Art's Sake' by Michael Watts. As part of a promotional tour Fagen and Becker travelled to London and gave interviews at Melody Maker and The BBC. This Melody Maker piece was perhaps the most illuminating feature on Steely Dan in the 1970's.

Rolling Stone 7/1/76 p.66-
Ken Tucker reviews The Royal Scam and calls Steely Dan "a lovable perverse bunch"

Stereo Review 8/76 p. 80-
'The Only Thing Outrageous About This Group is its Name' by Stephen Holden. While acknowledging that *The Royal Scam* is a good album Holden insists on trashing the group Steely Dan.

Winnipeg Free Press 8/18/76-
'Steely Dan's rock is sinister' by George Kanzler (Newhouse News Service) Critic Kanzler declares that Stely Dan is "a phantom group exploring a netherworld of druggy paranoia."

Newsweek 8/23/76
'Recluse Rock' by Janet Maslin w/ Dewey Graham. Brief article noting Steely Dan members reclusive nature. Includes an interesting photo of Becker and Fagen jamming in a Malibu bungalo.

New Times 8/76 –
includes brief talk with ex-drummer Jim Hodder

The Derrick-Oil City (PA) 12/16/76
'The Best Rock of Past Year' by Abe Peck (AP) Peck declares that Steely Dan is, "What Patti Smith would sound like if she stayed in school."

Music Gig 12/76
'Steely Dan Talks At Last' by Helen Shapiro

Steely Dan File Appendixes

1977

New Times 2//18/77 p.45

'Fancy Dan' by Arthur Lubow. Interesting piece which includes comments by William S. Burroughs and an early publicity photo of Becker and Fagen sleaning on a pool table.

Music Gig 5/77

'Steely Dan Hit The Road'. Article that announces plans for Steely Dan's planned 1977 US tour which never materialized.

Melody Maker 9/17/77-

extensive review of the yet to be released *Aja*.

NY Times 10/9/77 (Entertainment Section)

'America's Finest Maybe-Rock Non-Band' by Robert Palmer. Excellent review of *Aja* which Becker calls "sound sculpture".

New Times 10/29/77-

'Steely Dan's Golden Aja'. Includes odd photo of Becker and Fagen at a supermarket.

High Fidelity 11/77-

'Steely Dan Sans Sarcasm' by Sam sutherland. A Steely Dan collectible as it is a rare piece that features them on the cover.

Rolling Stone 11/3/77 p.56

'Dazed At The Dude Ranch'

Rolling Stone 12/28/77 p.11-

'The Second Coming of Steely Dan' by Cameron Crowe. Features haunting photo later used in Greatest Hits.

The Steely Dan File

1978

News Record (Vermont) 4/28/78 p.54
'Writer-lyricist David Palmer explores madness in album' by Rex Rutkowski David Palmer talks about his new band Wha-Koo and his work with Carole King and Steely Dan.

Rolling Stone 4/6/78 –

'Thundering Herd Meets Steely Dan' by Mikal Gilmore. Brief piece on the Woody Herman collaboration.

United Press International 11/2/78-

'Steely Dan defies music establishment' by Bruce Meyer (UPI) Fagen and Becker discuss compiling the first greatest hit set for ABC Records

1979

Musician, Player & Listener 9/10/79-
'A Summer's Sunday Picnic with Steely Dan' by Jon Pareles. Features shots of Steely Dan in New York.

1980

Billboard 7/5/80-
notes legal dispute between Steely Dan and MCA.

Rolling Stone 9/4/80 p.29-
notes star-studded line-up for new Gaucho lp.

Variety 10/28/80-
'New Steely Dan Material Stays at MCA, For Now'. Article notes MCA Records legal victory in retaining rights to Gaucho.

Steely Dan File Appendixes

1981

Syracuse Herald Journal 1/5/81-
'1980's best pop music albums don't include usual favorites' by George Kanzler. Kanzler calls Steely Dan "masters of the ominous" and "their messages still the same sugar-coated cyanide".

Stereo Review 1/81-
'Too Good For The Common Folk' by Jon Pareles

Variey 2/3/81-
'Steely Dan's Becker Hit in suit over '80 Death'. Notes $17.5Million law suit waged by Lillian Wyshak against Becker for the drug overdose death of her daughter Karen Stanley at Becker NY apartment in January 1980. Suit was eventually settled out of court.

Billboard 2/28/81-
notes spat between Azoff and MCA over 'Time Out of Mind' flip side.

Musician, Player & Listener 3/81-
Steely Dan are featured on the cover and interviewed.

NY Times 6/15/81-
'Steely Dan duo going it alone' by Robert Palmer. In a brief interview, Fagen anounces his split with Becker and his plans to release a solo album.

1982

Warner Brothers Records-
October 1982. A publicity sheet announces that "no one will be able to tell the difference between this album (Fagen's solo album The Nightfly) and Steely Dan"

The Steely Dan File

1983
High Fidelity 1/83-
>Fagen interviewed about writing and recording of The Nightfly.

New Musical Express-
>3/83- Fagen is interviewed in London. He also does an interview with the BBC at this time.

1986
Billboard 6/86 -
>Rosie Vela: This Year's Model Artist' by Sharon Liveten Article notes Steely Dan crews help on Vela's Zazu album.

1987
Guitar For Practicing Musician 2/87 p.56-
>'Walter Becker of Steely Dan:Solid Art by John Stix. Becker's first US interview in six years. He recounts early recording sessions of 1972 and 1974 with Palmer, Baxter and Derringer.

1988
Newsday 11/29/88-
>After Steely Dan, Private Don' by Stephen Williams.-Inane piece with Fagen in which he announces once and for all that Steely Dan is no more and that Steely Dan music is "unpleasant to listen to."

1990
Newsday 4/7/90-
>'Donald Fagen and Friends' by Wayne Robins. A review of one of the first NY Rock and Soul Revue concerts at the Beacon.

San Francisco Examiner 6/16/90-
>'Jimmy Hodder Ex-Steely Dan drummer'.Notes drowning death of original Steely Dan member Jim Hodder at 42.

Steely Dan File Appendixes

Billboard 6/16/90-
> 'Former Steely Dan Cohorts Combine Skills at Hit Factory' by Jesse Nash and George Flowers. Article on Becker and Fagen recording sessions in NY for upcoming Fagen solo lp.

1991

Billboard 10/2/91-
> 'Walter Becker Steels Production Spotlight' by Suzan Nunziata. Article on Becker's work with Fagen and his work for Triloka Records with engineer Roger Nichols.

1992

Billboard 2/1/92-
> Fagen, Katz Going with the Flow of River Sound" by Suzan Nunziata. Profiles the River Sound Recording Studios recently purchased by Katz and Fagen.

1993

Billboard 4/2/93-
> Donald Fagen's Epic Kamakiriad" by Timothy White. High praise for Fagen's new solo lp from Billboard's editor

Musician 9/93-
> 'The Return of Steely Dan' cover feature.

Jazziz Magazine 9/93-
> cover feature on Donald Fagen

San Francisco 9/14/93-
> A critical review of Steely Dan's Mountain View, California concert by Joel Selvin

Citizen Steely Dan booklet 11/93-
> filled with old photos and critical barbs from 1970's record reviews.

The Steely Dan File

1994

Billboard 8/26/94-
> interview with Becker on his new solo lp.

Guitar Player 12/94 p.63-
> 'The Whacky World of Walter Becker' by Chris Gill. An interview with Becker is complimented by a study of three of Steely Dan's greatest guitar solos (Exploring three Steely Dan Solos by Jesse Gress); Do It Again, Rikki Don't Lose That Number and Black Friday

Reeling In The Years Omnibus Press UK by Brian Sweet-
> 200 page book by British fan Sweet, the originator of the Metal Leg fanzine; includes input from Denny Dias and Gary Katz but no input from either Becker or Fagen..

1995

Rolling Stone 12/14/95 p.86-
> Critic Greg Kot calls Alive in America a 'pointless Document'.

Mojo 12/95-
> 'The Return of Steely Dan'. Hilarious interview that recounts the entire Steely Dan saga.

1996

San Francisco Examiner 8/13/96-
> Q & A with Steely Dan. Brief interview about Steely Dan's Art Crimes Tour of '96.

Steely Dan File Appendixes

2000

Guardian, Manchester (UK); Jan 14, 2000; pg. 16-
'Countdown to Ecstasy:Librarians on acid' by Barney Hoskyns

Billboard, New York; Jan 15, 2000; pg. 15-
Giant's Steely Dan does it again on disc; Carla Hay

Entertainment Weekly, New York; Mar 3, 2000,pg. 34-
The band with 2 brains; Jeff Gordinier;

Chicago Sun - Times, Chicago, Ill.; Mar 5, 2000; pg. 19-
Steely Dan does it again after 20-year hiatus; By Steve Morse

Rolling Stone, New York; Mar 30, 2000, pg. 32-
Return of the dark brothers; Alec Wilkinson;

San Francisco Chronicle, Jun 8, 2000; pg. E.1`-
'Old School' Is Back in Session With Steely Dan / Veteran rockers reel off their hits in Concord; James Sullivan

Daily News, Los Angeles, Calif.; Jun 15, 2000; pg. L-
Static-Free:Steely Dan Sneers, Leers Through 20 Years of its Classics by Fred Shuster

Times Union, Albany, N.Y.; Jun 29, 2000; pg. P.10
'Comfort zone Steely Dan's road trip highlights combination of genres' by Greg Haymes;

The Guardian, Manchester (UK); Sep 11, 2000; pg. 18
'Outsiders' night in: Steely Dan Wembley Arena by John L Walters;

The Steely Dan File

2001

Chicago Sun - Times, Feb 22, 2001; pg. 42
'Steely Dan beats rap at Grammys' by Jim DeRogatis;

The Christian Science Monitor; May 18, 2001; pg. 17-
'Steely Dan: reelin' in the accolades' by Stephen Humphries

2003

Syracuse Post Standard 9/2/2003-
'Steely Dan remains razor Sharp', by Mark Bialczak

2004

Chicago Daily Herald 2/8/2004-
Cornelius Bumpus Obituary

2006

SF Chronicle 3/30/2006–

'No static at all - Donald Fagen's sound as sleek as it's ever been' by Joel Selvin

Steely Dan File Appendixes

Steely Dan online

For current information on Steely Dan check out these websites

www.steelydan.com

www.donaldfagen.com

www.walterbecker.com

About the Author-
A native of Babylon, Long Island in New York, Stephen V. O'Rourke studied broadcasting in New York City and earned a BA in Media Studies at the University of South Australia. A Steely Dan fan since his teenage years O'Rourke has used their music as a soundtrack to his life journeys. A longtime resident of the San Francisco area he now lives in Singapore with his wife, Rina Ong (an educator and part-time actress), his two sons Charlie and Jack and their dog Scruffy.

www.ingramcontent.com/pod-product-compliance
Lightning Source LLC
Chambersburg PA
CBHW062214080426
42734CB00010B/1880